Eva-Maria Krämer

Get to Know
Dog Breeds

The 200 Most Popular Breeds

Contents

Sheepdogs

Bred to guard
and round up
the herd working
as a team with
the shepherd

Cattle Dogs and Farm Dogs

Bred to herd
livestock to the
market or guard
the yard

Herding Dogs

Bred to guard
and protect herds
independently

Gundogs With Handlers

Bred to forage,
track, and retrieve
working together
with the hunter

Dogs

‹ **The wolf—the ancestor of all dogs**

› About This Book

When I first began to study dog breeds in their countries of origin in the seventies, and, whenever possible, to witness them performing the duties they were bred to do, I found their work and life circumstances and their relationships with their people to be very impressive. Consequently, it became clear to me that there wasn't a dog book devoted specifically to this topic. The authors more or less described the appearance of the dog, but they hardly touched on the background of the breed. And this could mean all the difference between a wonderful experience or a terrible disappointment for life with your dog.

This book profiles a broad range of pedigree dogs. It is primarily intended to help the owner decide what dog is best for his or her family. The photographs show typical specimens of each breed, which makes a detailed description of the appearance unnecessary. Any differences in fur type and color and the shoulder height are noted. Unlike in many other countries, cosmetic tail docking and ear cropping (clipping the tail and ears to make the dog look a certain way) are not illegal in the United States.

However, these surgical procedures are highly controversial. With the exception of some gundogs' tails, which are often docked for functional reasons, this book shows the dogs as nature intended—with ears and tails intact.

I have used a new approach in this book; I grouped the breeds according to the duties for which they were originally bred. This is not consistent with the official grouping by the Fédération Cynologique Internationale (FCI) [World Canine Organization based in Belgium]. I was inspired by the grouping used in Jan Nijboer's dog-training program, Natural Dogmanship®, which seemed to make more sense to me and was synonymous with my own experience. The description for each group will enable the reader to decide whether a certain type of dog breed would be suitable for his or her lifestyle or not. Any relevant discrepancies have also been noted for each breed.

› The Dog in Our Society

When I look back on my decades of life with dogs, it is easy to see that both people's living conditions and the role of the dog have changed. The inclusion of the dog in the family home and lifestyle is a relatively new concept. Before this, dogs only rarely shared a home with their owners, and life outdoors was typical, particularly for large breeds. People trained their dogs using traditional methods, and animal behavioral science was only in the very early stages. This new way of living with the dog caused conflict in a situation that previously did not exist. Nowadays we have dogs living with us in our homes that instinctively feel the need to perform their duties but are unable to carry them out. In our own "den," we give the dog a role as a responsible pack member, but at the same time train him to be subordinate.

We tend to look at the dog as a family member, often like another child in the house, and cherish and care for him in this way. Yet conversely, more and more often one hears of a new concept in our society—the canine behavioral problem. In reality, it is often the human who is the cause of this problem. Dogs have been robbed of their natural duties and placed in a pack whose language and culture they do not understand; they are expected to obey, not break anything, and pursue the same interests as us, often only having one or two walks a day, and are forced to endure endless periods of rest in the home.

Real problem dogs are rare; most problems are only seen as such from the human's point of view, but for the dog, this so-called problem behavior is seen as normal. What one finds fun is intolerable for the other! When an owner is able to understand why a dog behaves in a certain way, he or she will be able to deal with the dog far better, or perhaps consider a different breed altogether. Appearance is really not important. If you have a good relationship with your dog, then to you, he will be the most beautiful dog in the world. The purpose of this book is to ensure that you and your dog live happily ever after.

‹ During the journey from wolf to pedigree dog, our dogs have undergone many environmental changes.

ᴠ You know which characteristics and skills to expect from a pedigree dog.

› Why a Pedigree Dog?

The dog was the first animal to be domesticated, and humans have largely shaped his development. Early humans bred dogs for a specific purpose. It is difficult to determine how important the appearance of a dog was in very early breeding. Breeds with a predetermined breed standard, as is the case for all pedigree breeds today, have only been in existence for about one hundred fifty years. This is a relatively small amount of time throughout canine breeding history.

A great advantage of owning a pedigree is that you as the owner will already have a good idea what he will look like and how he will behave. As a "product of nature," there will always be minor differences to a dog's individual appearance and personality, and there is no such thing as a perfect example of the breed. The breeder's aim is to get as close as possible to this ideal, and achieve uniformity within a particular breed.

For this reason, breeders will attend dog shows where their dogs are measured and assessed according to their standard, or participate in performance tests. Anyone who has an idea about which breed they would like to own in the future can get a good feel for this breed by going to one of these shows. The mixed-breed dog, however, is a "surprise package" in every respect, and is in no way healthier or less problematic than a purebred; this is especially true when it comes to the modern trend of commercial breeders who cross popular breeds and advertise them in the classified section of daily newspapers. Buying a dog out of pity and bringing strays into your home are often associated with many difficulties. Good will alone is not enough in these cases! Not every dog will find it easy to adjust to life in a new household.

Another great advantage of owning a pedigree dog is the help owners receive from breed kennel clubs; these clubs offer support and advice and also sporting and social activities. The objective of each kennel club is to monitor breeding practices in accordance with animal welfare, preserve the purity of the breed, and also maintain the standard of the breed. For this purpose, breeding rules were created, as well as preventive health care measures. Only breeders who follow these rules to the letter are permitted to register their puppies with the appropriate kennel club.

In recent years, pedigree dog breeding has come under fire—not without good reason. When some people smell a moneymaking opportunity, they will not shy away from employing the worst practices. Puppies that are bred en masse for profit, an operation known as a puppy mill, have had no breed-specific rearing and are often mentally disturbed and ill. It is the buyer's responsibility to inform himself or herself properly, and he or she must not support this kind of breeding by making a hasty purchase.

› Choosing a Dog

First answer the following questions:
- › Does my family have the time and space for a dog?
- › Will my family be able to understand and deal with our dog's needs?
- › Can my family afford to own a dog?
- › Who will look after the dog when we go on vacation?
- › Will the landlord allow us to keep a dog?
- › Can my family commit to keeping a dog for its entire life (ten to fifteen years)?
- › Will my "dream dog" be suitable for my family's lifestyle?

You will find valuable resources in the Further Reading section on page 157 to help you answer all these questions. As for the dog itself, the appearance alone should not be the deciding factor. You will also need to consider the dog's characteristics, exercise requirements, and daily care.

› Long-Haired or Short-Haired Breed?

The length of the dog's fur could play a part in your choice of dog. Generally speaking, short-haired dogs with no undercoat are more weather sensitive than long-haired dogs with a dense, insulating undercoat. Dogs with short fur shed less, but the fur tends to stick stubbornly to clothes and other materials, while dogs with an undercoat shed twice a year in great

◀ Think about personality, not just appearance, when deciding on the right dog for you.

▾ Male or female? That is the question!

clumps that will spread all over the house. Long fur is not always maintenance intensive, but you may have to groom your dog daily with lots of love and care to keep him looking clean and well maintained.

Any loose fur can be brushed out; however, the main issue is that very long-haired dogs will bring a lot of dirt into the house. Breeds that are regularly trimmed or shorn are much easier to keep clean, but professional grooming can be expensive.

▸ Male or Female?

The question of gender comes up frequently. Contrary to popular opinion, males are less complicated than females because they are subjected to less hormonal changes. However, they will forget everything you have ever taught them when tracking the scent of a female in heat. Anyone who travels a lot, does a lot of sports, and spends time with lots of different dogs is better off with a male dog. They tend to be easier to socialize, despite the reputation for being more aggressive. If you find that your male dog is particularly dominant, it may help to get him neutered.

A female will usually come into season every six months, but her hormones will subject her to some interesting changes a few weeks in advance. She will become unfocused, sometimes experience a change in her nature, and must be well protected during the heat cycle, which lasts three weeks, in order to avoid unwanted puppies. The hormone levels will then balance out again, or she may have a pseudo pregnancy, which will delay the process by six to eight weeks. Spaying your female is one way to avoid these hormonal changes, but an operation under general anesthetic does have associated risks. In any case, she should be treated with extra care during the hormonal dips between heat cycles. I personally would not recommend hormone treatments. Spaying and neutering must only be performed by a licensed veterinarian.

Gender does not have an effect on the sociability of some breeds. I have noted this in some of the breed descriptions. Female dogs are in no way inferior to male dogs. They are generally more prepared to submit and much less willing to fight over their ranking within the family pack.

▸ The Right Breeder

Please contact the kennel club of the breed you feel is most suited to you, and go to as many events as possible so you can get to know the breed and the people involved. Have your parents help you get addresses for breeders in your area, even if they are currently not breeding any puppies. A breeder who truly cares about her dog breed will be on hand to give you advice. Have your family visit some breeders, and ultimately make sure you purchase a puppy from a breeder who meets your expectations. The puppies should have enjoyed plenty of human contact and should show confidence around people. It is also important that you get along well with the breeder and understand the value of having contact beyond the sale. The breeder should be available to give you advice even after you have taken your dog home. Do not be surprised if the breeder asks you a lot of questions because she will want to make sure her puppies are going to good homes.

< A good breeder should provide her puppies with a variety of environmental stimulation and plenty of contact with children.

∨ No matter the breed, there is a training method for each one. Below is dog trainer Jan Nijboer who developed the Natural Dogmanship® program.

The breeder may add a clause in the sale contract. Usually, even after the sale, the welfare of these puppies will still be a matter close to her heart. If she discourages you from taking on a puppy from a particular breed, then you should be thankful that she may have saved you a lot of trouble.

Responsible dog breeding is expensive and complicated. Pedigree puppies can cost hundreds and even thousands of dollars. Beware of cheaper puppies! Reputable breeders usually do not have any trouble selling their puppies. The puppies should not be anxious or aggressive if they have been bred in an ideal environment. Of course, every dog will bark at a stranger, but by copying the friendly manner of the breeder, the puppy will eventually calm down in the presence of people he does not know. If the dog cannot be controlled by spoken orders, that is a sign of a problem! Do not burden yourself with a dog that is nervous about his environment or sees people as a threat. Do not accept any excuses or apologies from the breeder and move on to the next breeder.

> The Right Breed

When choosing a breed, keep in mind that very large dogs usually have a relatively short life expectancy. Furthermore, you should make sure that the puppy

is not the result of inbreeding (mating two dogs that are closely related). This method is used all too often to provide the desired features quickly and without too much effort. Unfortunately certain undesirable traits will also be evident. Look at the pedigree papers and check whether the ancestors names have appeared several times in the first five generations. Inbreeding may make sense when pioneering a new dog breed in order to achieve the desired image for the breed, but genetic diversity should then be maintained for optimal results in terms of health, fitness, strength, endurance, longevity, and fertility in order for breeding to be successful in the long run. If a breeder has a good reason to undertake inbreeding, then she should also bear the responsibility of these puppies and not burden the new puppy owner.

> Being child friendly is not a characteristic dogs are born with; it is the result of influence and upbringing.

Some breeds do suffer from inherited diseases, many times because they have been inbred too often. Check with the kennel club to see if there are any diseases associated with a particular breed. Usually breeding regulations are intended to be used as precautionary measures. This applies in particular for many dogs to prevent hip dysplasia, a painful joint condition, from occurring. The breeding animals of affected breeds must be x-rayed. It is recommended that you buy a puppy with healthy parents that have received good nutrition and plenty of exercise, which reduces the likelihood of disease. I have purposely left out breed-specific diseases and defects because it is usually just a few dogs affected nowadays; appropriate breeding combats these problems today, meaning a healthy litter of puppies tomorrow. No one can guarantee eternal health. Responsible breeders should breed to the best of their knowledge and only use healthy dogs with perfect temperaments for breeding.

> Family-Friendly Dogs

I realize that with any breed, the issue of child friendliness is always mentioned. Dogs and humans have been living together successfully for many millennia. Children and dogs have always been a happy team, and humans have lived for thousands of years with the knowledge that it is acceptable for an animal to defend itself. Nowadays, owners are taken to court and ordered to put down a dog that bites; this has caused some breeds to be labeled as dangerous. Of course I condemn those who abuse dogs, force other people to live in fear and terror,

or make their dogs fight for money. But dogs that do not bite do not exist. It is simply a defense mechanism—just as we humans use our fists. Whether the dog uses this mechanism depends on temperament, life experience, and the situation the dog finds himself in. How child friendly a dog is depends on how the parents deal with the dog when around the child. Children need to learn how to deal with dogs and vice versa. The responsibility lies with the parents.

Of course a toy-sized dog is less dangerous than a big dog simply because her bite causes less damage. Parents should always supervise children and dogs together. A family with both a toddler and a dog will need plenty of time, space, and knowledge of canine behavior to keep the situation under control. Having a dog is like having another toddler, and you should not underestimate how much work a dog can be for her family. It is important that you meet the needs of a particular breed and make sure she fits in with your family.

Sheepdogs

Left: When herding, the German shepherd always keeps the shepherd in view.

Right: In the vast countryside of Scotland, the border collie drives the sheep from one pasture to another.

Far right: The Malinois is always on the go.

Next page, bottom: The Australian shepherd is a very smart breed.

Anyone who has observed a dog herding sheep and watched documentaries about wolves in the wild will recognize that herding is hunting. So why do we find sheepdogs to be such excellent companions? Because they hunt in packs, just like we humans would have done thousands of years ago. Working as a team enables predators to hunt larger prey. Wolves generally hunt larger prey in the winter when there are not many smaller animals available. They join together to form a large group and pursue the herds. In order to hunt successfully, they define each role clearly within the pack and communicate clearly with each other; failure to do so could mean death for members of the pack. Each animal willingly takes his place and performs according to his best talent. The various sheepdog breeds have many different talents. There are clear rules for each

hunt: the pack leader determines the beginning and the strategy of the hunt. Then a lightning-fast response is required from the rest of the pack. Each dog knows exactly what he has to do in order to contribute to the success of the hunt. He plays his role instinctively, and then he leaves the last step, the killing of the prey, to the pack leader; in this case, the shepherd.

The physical and behavioral characteristics of sheepdogs largely depend on the landscape and climate; this is reflected in the different breeds. In fertile lowlands, sheep graze on fallow land, land that has not been seeded. The shepherd and his dog monitor the herd to make sure that only a certain area of the land is grazed. Close cooperation, attentiveness, high level of endurance, and guarding against thieves and intruders are all qualities of a sheepdog. Sheepdogs on

heathlands and steppes accompany large herds, but the work is more independent, and the dog has to use his own initiative. On barren hills, sheep graze vast areas without supervision, so the sheepdog must independently herd sheep or goats to the desired location.

due to training issues must be picked up on as soon as possible and can only be corrected with good knowledge and consistently good training. Sheepdogs have excellent hearing over long distances and can learn to understand the nuances of their master's different whistles and

Other typical characteristics of sheepdogs are good eyesight so that even the smallest movements can be seen in the distance; a prey drive for wildlife; strong social ties to his group; and a distrust of strangers. To ensure survival, he will make sure he knows his place in the pack and not fight with other dogs over ranking. These dogs feel safe and secure with a firm, loving pack leader and become mentally and physically disturbed if the pack leader disappears. They are therefore seen as "sensitive." This youthful willingness to be subordinate lasts well into old age; this dog loves playing and working together with his leader. Sheepdogs are working dogs; they need to be given tasks to do by their people and feel they are being physically and mentally utilized. Therefore, time spent working closely with his human is indispensable for the sheepdog. Any undesirable behavior

commands. These dogs tend to be very sensitive to noise. They are very fast, agile, persistent, and very good at jumping, which makes them ideal for any sporting endeavors. The territorial and sexual instinct is less pronounced than the hunting and herding instinct, which can make this a very pleasant family dog. The sheepdog is always alert and will readily bark to protect his family. He must be taught to behave in a friendly manner toward strangers.

A sheepdog with a close bond to his people does not enjoy hunting independently, which often leads people to think he does not like to hunt at all. In fact, he is a capable hunter but will not stray too far from his owner and can usually be called off scent tracks. Sadly, there are many underutilized and unattended sheepdogs, and these dogs exhibit some of the more serious behavioral problems.

German Shepherd

Shoulder height: 23.5–25.5 inches for a male, 21.5–23.5 inches for a female

Weight: 66–88 pounds for a male, 48.5–70.5 pounds for a female

Color: black, blackish brown in various shades, wolf gray

Coat: short-haired and long-haired varieties with undercoat

A robust, low-maintenance dog that sheds heavily

An avalanche rescue dog

At the end of the nineteenth century, this short-haired, wolflike breed was used in Germany as herding dogs, bred for use by the police and military. In both world wars, this breed was held in high esteem by soldiers and so established worldwide popularity. Unfortunately, over the last few decades there has been a discrepancy between performance dogs for dog sports and working dogs, and so-called beauty breeding; these exaggerated aesthetic ideals have harmed this breed's health and character. German shepherds from responsible breeders are still outstanding service dogs and reliable sports and family dogs. The German shepherd needs close contact with his owner and should be given plenty of exercise and meaningful tasks. Every German shepherd dog owner will be able to find a suitable activity for his dog, such as dog tournaments, agility, disaster rescue, avalanche rescue, assistance, herding, and guiding the visually impaired. Under no circumstance should the German shepherd be misused as a watchdog for the house. The wrong activities and training will have a negative impact on this spirited dog that was born to be a working dog. He is not really recommended to be purely just a companion dog for the family.

White Swiss Shepherd

Shoulder height: 23.5–26 inches for a male, 21.5–24 inches for a female

Weight: 66–88 pounds for a male, 55–77 pounds for a female

Color: white

Coat: long-haired and short-haired varieties

This breed is known as the American-Canadian white sheepdog by the FCI.

When German shepherds were purebred at the end of the nineteenth century, white examples of this breed were already known but not very popular. Because the gene for the white coat (not albino) is still present, occasionally colored parents will have white puppies. In the United States, they are pedigrees according to the American Kennel Club (AKC), but the breed standard states that their color is a mistake, and they have no chance at dog shows when compared to standard colored dogs. White shepherds are usually bred by enthusiasts who have no wish to be involved in the major competitions that are based on physical appearance and performance. The first white shepherd dogs appeared in Switzerland. Some canine organizations, such as the German Shepherd Club of Germany (SV), do not recognize the white color. However, the breed has been officially registered and bred in other countries. The Swiss Canine Society (SKG) requested recognition from the FCI. This breed's nature corresponds with that of the German shepherd, but it is somewhat more sensitive. This dog's physique is that of the original German shepherd. He is a popular family pet.

A disaster rescue dog at work

13

Belgian Shepherd

Shoulder height: 23.5–26 inches for a male, 22–24.5 inches for a female

Weight: 55–66 pounds for a male, 44–55 pounds for a female

Belgian shepherds are among the best-known service dogs.

Developed in Belgium at the end of the nineteenth century, this breed is a medium-sized, agile, determined, vigilant shepherd dog with a protective instinct, a strong bond with his owner, yet also able to work independently if the situation requires. In 1891, Professor A. Reul took on the breeding of these sheepdogs and advanced the pedigree.

The FCI divides the Belgium shepherd into four subgroups according to color and fur type, while the AKC recognizes them as four separate breeds. The four varieties are

Groenendael: black, long hair; developed in the village of Groenendael

Tervuren: long hair, reddish brown, black fur tips, and black mask; named after the village of Tervuren

Malinois: short hair, fawn with black coat and black mask; from the Malines area

Laekenois: coarse hair, color same as Malinois; named after a coarse-haired breed of sheepdog in the Laeken area.

Belgian shepherds are very good family dogs and tireless leisure companions. They are intelligent, keen to work, docile, vigilant, and suitable for a variety of training methods. They need a lot of exercise and tasks to keep them occupied and show great talent in anything from agility to disaster rescue training.

**Previous page, top:
a Tervuren**

**Previous page, bottom:
a Groenendael**

Left: a Malinois

Below: a Laekenois

The Malinois breed is becoming more commonly used by police and customs. Dogs bred to perform specific duties are not recommended as family dogs. Belgian shepherds are very sensitive and should be raised in an empathic and loving way. Therefore, they are recommended only conditionally for the inexperienced dog owner. The Laekenois is calmer and quieter than his very temperamental, more agile cousins. He is no less talented but unfortunately rarely encountered. All fur types are easy to care for.

The Belgian shepherd is distinguished by his bubbly temperament and perpetual readiness for action—a fact that should not be underestimated! Physically, but above all mentally, under-utilized dogs can show signs of many behavioral problems. Owners must spend a lot of time with this breed. A simple bike ride will not be enough.

Dutch Shepherd

Shoulder height: 22.5–24.5 inches for a male, 21.5–23.5 for a female

Weight: about 62 pounds for a male, about 51 pounds for a female.

Color: dark brown or gray with light brindle

The brindle coat pattern used to be found in German shepherds as well.

Dutch, Belgian, and German shepherds are closely related. However, Dutch shepherds never acquired a huge popularity and were not bred as profusely as the German shepherd. Even in their home country, they are overshadowed by the world-famous German shepherd and the colorful Belgian shepherds. Therefore, this breed has retained the original sheepdog type. The short-haired type is the most common, followed by the coarse-haired variety. The long-haired type is very rarely bred. The long-haired variety has a more sensitive nature than his short-haired and coarse-haired cousins. This breed is known to be a reliable family dog. However, he also works as a guide dog, customs dog, and police dog. The Dutch shepherd needs a close bond with his owner. He is mistrustful of strangers but loyal to his family. His natural protective instinct makes him a good guard dog. He loves to work, needs consistent leadership, and is a good choice for a new dog owner. He loves to exercise, is easy to care for, and is well suited to dog sports and agility tournaments. All three fur types are easy to maintain.

Top: a short-haired Dutch shepherd

Left: a long-haired Dutch shepherd

Old German Shepherd

The shoulder height, weight, color, and other characteristics are not bred according to a particular standard. The shoulder height is estimated to be between 20 to 24 inches.

Some types of Old German shepherds are suitable as family dogs if their zeal and their intelligence are used in the right way.

Due to the pure breeding of German shepherds, the older breed fell into oblivion. This breed was only kept going in the former German Democratic Republic (also known as East Germany when the country was divided by the Berlin Wall). When sheep farmers began to work again after the Berlin Wall came down in 1990, older breeds of sheepdog came under threat. The German association devoted to breeding Old German shepherds (AHH) promotes the breeding of the older breeds, not for beauty but for their skills as sheepdogs. The impact of climate and terrain means that these dogs vary widely in size, body type, coat texture, and temperament. They are divided into several subgroups: the schafpudel ("sheep poodle"), which has wavy fur; the Harzer fox dog; the Siegerländer fox dog; the Westerwald Kuhhund, which is medium sized and has long, fox-red fur; the gelbbacke, a medium-sized, long-haired, black-and-red dog; the black, long-haired variety; the tiger, which describes all types with the merle pattern; the Strobel, which is mostly black with dense, coarse hair; and the stumper, which describes all types born with a stumpy tail.

Top: a Harzer fox dog

Bottom left: the schafpudel

Bottom right: an example of the tiger variety

17

Collie (Rough)

Shoulder height: 22–24 inches for a male, 20–22 inches for a female

Weight: 50–75 pounds

Color: sable with white, tricolored, and blue merle with white

According to the American Kennel Club standards, the male can be up to 26 inches, and the female can be up to 24 inches.

The collie's ancestors were brought from England to Scotland as shepherd dogs. Queen Victoria's love of Scottish sheepdogs and new canine beauty contests spurred breeders to breed elegant collies in a variety of delightful colors. The first collies were used during wartimes as medical response dogs and messenger dogs. The crossing with Borzoi dogs changed this creature from an agile farm dog into a serene, sophisticated family pet. Thanks to the canine superstar Lassie, the breed became extremely popular in the sixties. The collie is adaptable, family oriented, willing to please, and intelligent. Unfortunately, owners do not always make the most of her capabilities. She is suitable as a rescue, tracking, and herding dog as well as being ideal for agility tournaments. She is playful well into old age, always alert, and ready to defend in case of emergency. At the moment, breeding trends lean toward overly dense, care-intensive fur, which is not really typical of the breed, and this should be taken into consideration if you are thinking about owning one of these dogs. Typical collie fur is easy to care for and dirt resistant. The collie is a good beginner dog with an innate sociability. She needs consistent leadership and can be kept in a group of two or more.

Collie (Smooth)

Shoulder height: 22–24 inches for a male, 20–22 inches for a female

Weight: 45–65 pounds for a male, 40–55 pounds for a female

Color: sable with white, tricolored, and blue merle with white

Merle is an ancient herding dog color, not a recent trend.

The smooth-haired collie is an old British working dog breed. Thomas Bewick, the famous English wood engraver, kept these dogs as working dogs in 1790. To this day, farmers still prefer to own a short-haired dog that does not suffer during the hot summer months. At the early stage of development, these dogs were paraded in the show ring, but unlike the rough collie, the smooth collie's real purpose was to be an all-around farm dog. She has a wiry figure, self-confidence, and a healthy dose of courage, which she draws on when herding bulls. However, she has always lived in the shadow of her long-haired cousin and, for some time, was in danger of becoming extinct. Today, with her lovely temperament, great intelligence, and love of work, this elegant dog is growing in popularity. She is more agile and powerful than the rough collie and needs consistent leadership with plenty of meaningful tasks. She has proved herself as an excellent disaster rescue dog and assistance dog for people with disabilities. She excels at dog sports. The short, weatherproof coat is easy to care for but sheds heavily. Any loose hair can easily be brushed out and also removed from any material. Her standard description is the same as that of the rough collie, besides the coat of course. As a breed in her own right, she is no longer allowed to be crossbred with the rough collie.

Border Collie

Shoulder height: 21 inches for a male, females are somewhat smaller

Weight: 25–55 pounds

Color: many colors, never mostly white

This dog was bred as a show dog in Australia and New Zealand.

The border collie comes from the border region between England and Scotland, simply known as the Borders. She has a unique way of working; when herding, she assumes a crouched stance, keeping her eyes fixed on the sheep. She works under the command of the shepherd and responds to whistles, calls, or hand signals over many miles, as well as in the sheep pen, where independent work is required if the shepherd is busy with the sheep. The border collie's love of work as well as her willingness to be subordinate are innate behaviors. She has a great temperament and incredible stamina. Her intelligence is superior to many other breeds. She does not like to be inactive. Despite her willingness to please and low cost to keep, this is a demanding dog that wants to be useful, whether on the farm or as a mountain rescue dog, disaster rescue dog, or tracking dog. She is extremely agile and obedient, so she is very well suited to dog sports. But even high-performance sports are not enough. If her zeal for work is not satisfied, she will become a difficult pet. Unfortunately, she has been marketed as a fashion dog, and many puppies become problem dogs in the hands of owners who do not know the breed well.

Australian Shepherd

Shoulder height: 20–23 inches for a male, 18–21 inches for a female

Weight: 50–65 for a male, 40–55 for a female

Color: blue merle, red merle, black, or red with or without white and/or tan markings

The miniature Australian shepherd is 12 to 18 inches tall at the shoulders and very sporty.

Sheep farmers from the United Kingdom, France, and Spain took their sheepdogs with them to their new home in the United States. The Australian shepherd, or Aussie, was crossbred with collies and dingoes to give her greater strength and endurance. Dogs were exchanged at livestock markets—meeting places of shepherds and ranchers. They developed a strong, enormously persistent sheep and cattle dog bred for duties on a small farm or large ranch. The Aussie guards poultry and sheep and herds the dairy cattle and half-wild cattle to be mounted by cowboys. She also helps in dealing with the cattle during transportation. She is spirited, persistent, sociable, alert, and ready for action. This dog is easy to train and learns quickly. She will, however, need strong leadership and meaningful tasks or she will exhibit the same problematic behavior as an underutilized border collie. For this reason, she is a very demanding dog that needs an active, sporty owner and is happiest on a farm. She is a popular companion dog for horse riders because she does not stray too far. The sleek, long fur is easy to maintain.

Shetland Sheepdog

Shoulder height: 14.5 inches for a male, 14 inches for a female

Weight: 14–27 pounds

Color: sable, tricolor, blue merle (with and without tan markings), black and white, black and tan, all white markings

Also known as Shelties, these dogs are very sociable and happy to live in a group.

The Sheltie was the original farm and sheepdog on the Shetland Islands, famous for its small sheep, cattle, and ponies. The Sheltie guarded the yard, protected gardens and fields from voracious sheep, and kept down the numbers of rats and mice. These small dogs were tough, smart, agile, quick, and obedient. Sailors bought them home as souvenirs for their families. Shelties were crossed with dwarf spaniels, papillons, and Pomeranians to create pretty, colorful dogs. Later they were crossed with collies to improve the breed. The Sheltie is eager to learn, friendly, and a reliable guard dog. She loves exercise and work. She is completely devoted to her owner and follows his every step. She is quite aloof with strangers. She is an ideal travel companion for people who are happy to take their pets everywhere with them. Strict, overly tough people are unsuitable for this sensitive dog. The spirited, hardworking Shelties are good jumpers, making them among the best canine agility athletes ever seen. Their sleek long fur is easy to care for but needs to be thoroughly brushed once a week.

Pyrenean Sheepdog

Shoulder height: *long-haired:* 16–19 inches for a male, 15–18 inches for a female; *smooth-faced:* 16–21 inches for a male, 16–20.5 inches for a female

Weight: 15–30 pounds

Color: fawn to reddish brown, black or gray, harlequin varieties

This breed originated in France.

As a typical mountain sheepdog, the **long-haired Pyrenean sheepdog** herds sheep and goats in the Pyrenees in mountain areas out of human reach. The obedient, lively dog works with admirable speed, endurance, and assertiveness. He is considered an excellent guard dog that is quick to defend but does not bark persistently. He is mistrustful of strangers. With his family, however, he is a devoted housemate. When working, he uses his own initiative, which gives him a special charm, and he requires consistent leadership. Thanks to his intelligence, he is very easy to train and will want to do everything with you. He always likes to know what is going on. He loves to be outdoors, is robust, and has a long life expectancy. This is a dog for active people. His fur needs occasional brushing so it does not mat.

The much less common **smooth-faced Pyrenean sheepdog** is easier to maintain but less spirited. This larger dog is kept by people who live at the base of the Pyrenees and herds flocks of sheep and other livestock.

A smooth-faced Pyrenean sheepdog

23

Bearded Collie

Shoulder height: 21–22 inches for a male, 20–21 inches for a female

Weight: 40–60 pounds

Color: slate gray, fawn, black, blue; all shades of gray, brown, or fawn with or without white markings

This dog has to learn to be obedient during grooming, right from puppyhood.

Nowadays this breed seldom performs the tasks for which he was originally bred. As a typical Scottish sheepdog of the mountain regions, he drove the sheep from the mountains into the valleys, keeping the herd together. This breed would almost certainly have become extinct if it had not been rediscovered purely by chance. A dedicated breeder in the early 1950s searched the United Kingdom high and low to find the right type of dogs to recreate this breed. The rustic, shaggy sheepdog became a coiffed beauty and conquered the world. The popularity of the "beardie" is largely due to his adorable nature. Unlike the typical sheepdog, he is open minded, even to strangers, and is friendly toward other animals too. This means he does not make a very good guard dog! He has a lively, sometimes noisy, loving temperament but needs very consistent leadership because his roguish charm is one that needs controlling. Beardies are extremely sensitive; they seem to sense their human's every emotion. The bearded collie takes up a lot of time, his care is complex, and he needs a lot of exercise and meaningful tasks. He is not a dog for people who lead inactive lifestyles.

Schapendoes

Shoulder height: 17–19.5 inches for a male, 16–18.5 inches for a female

Weight: 30–50 pounds

Color: all colors permitted

From 1971 onward, no further alterations were made to this breed. Before this, the Schapendoes was crossbred with non-pedigrees.

In 1940, the Dutch breeder P.M.C. Toepoel discovered the Schapendoes on the heath areas when cataloging dog breeds in Holland. Throughout the country, typical examples were brought together, examined, and used to further the breed. Experienced breeders and geneticists built up the breed again. This good-natured, outdoor-loving dog has won plenty of fans. The Schapendoes is a friendly, playful, lively family dog. He is alert but not aggressive. In the home, he is calm and never nervous, provided he is given enough exercise and meaningful tasks. The spirited, hardworking dog is very good for equestrian sport and agility sports. He will do anything for his master, but he needs to understand what and why. Working independently is in his blood; he will obey, but he is not reliant on commands. The

Schapendoes is compatible with other dogs. Grooming the dog when he is young is time consuming, but once his fur becomes coarser in adulthood, he only needs a thorough brushing every two weeks.

Polish Lowland Sheepdog

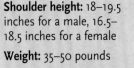

Shoulder height: 18–19.5 inches for a male, 16.5–18.5 inches for a female

Weight: 35–50 pounds

Color: all colors permitted, including patches

Some dogs are born with a stubby tail; this version is not permitted to be bred.

Pure breeding of this traditional sheepdog from the lowlands of Poland began in the 1940s. Dog enthusiasts wanted to further this breed and persuaded farmers and shepherds to supply their working dogs for breeding. This prevented the breed from becoming extinct. This sincere, genuine dog needs a lot of work and exercise; he works outdoors, whatever the weather, and is a reliable, energetic protector of the home. He has little propensity for straying. He is suspicious of strangers but is generally not aggressive or snappy. This dominant character, spirited into old age, needs consistent leadership because he will only give in to the leader of the pack; his resilient personality makes him difficult for an inexperienced dog owner. The coarse fur typical of the breed standard needs regular brushing. The effortless gait and delightful colors of this stocky, muscular dog are what make him so distinctive.

Portuguese Sheepdog and Catalonian Sheepdog

Portuguese Sheepdog (bottom)

Shoulder height: 18–21.5 inches for a male, 16.5–20.5 inches for a female

Weight: 26.5–39.5 pounds

Color: yellow, brown, gray, fawn, wolf-gray, and black, tan markings

Catalonian Sheepdog (left)

Shoulder height: 18.5–21.5 inches for a male, 18–21 inches for a female

Weight: 35–40 pounds

Color: brown, fawn, gray, and black with lighter markings

A relative of the bearded collie, Schapendoes, and the Polish lowland sheepdog

The Portuguese sheepdog comes from the south region of the Tagus River, near the Algarve (southernmost region of mainland Portugal), where he herds goats, sheep, pigs, and bulls. This dog is an old sheepdog breed with an excellent work ethic, temperament, and stamina. He is very alert and rather aloof with strangers but silly and affectionate toward his family. He is very docile but needs consistent leadership and a person whom he can accept as pack leader. Meaningful work is essential for this dog. His fur is similar to that of a goat's fur and must be brushed regularly.

The Catalonian sheepdog is the Spanish relative of the French Pyrenean sheepdog. He hails from the province of Catalonia, a region which extends to the Pyrenees and includes Barcelona. These mountain herders were not bred for their beauty but as robust, persistent working dogs. Therefore, the breed varies according to the region. The Catalonian sheepdog is docile, friendly, always on the move, and very alert. He is suspicious toward strangers. He is a rugged outdoor dog that requires a close family connection and plenty of meaningful tasks. The coarse coat needs occasional brushing.

Puli and Pumi

Puli (right and bottom left)

Shoulder height: 14–19 inches for a male, 13–18 inches for a female

Weight: 28.5–33 pounds for a male, 22–28.5 pounds for a female

Color: black, white, gray, fawn with black mask

Pumi (bottom right)

Shoulder height: 16–18.5 inches for a male, 15–17 inches for a female

Weight: 22–33 pounds for a male, 17.5–28.5 pounds for a female

Color: black, white, gray, fawn

Both breeds, the pumi more so than the puli, are lively, action-loving dogs.

Puli

The puli is an ancient sheepdog. She is extremely intelligent and learns quickly and eagerly. She carefully protects all members of her pack. The cheerful, always active dog fits in well on a farm or in a lively family. She is happy when she has a task to do and requires plenty of work and exercise. The fur is tightly curled and long, similar to dreadlocks. Combs and brushes are not ideal; the curled fur needs to be washed regularly for hygiene reasons. Shepherds shear these dogs every year along with the sheep. If an owner does not plan to exhibit his dog, the curls can be combed out or shaved, which makes life easier for both owner and dog.

Pumi

The pumi is a descendant of mixed breeds including the original wavy-haired sheepdog and is still often encountered as a working dog on a farm. It is thought that she has also been influenced by terrier and spitz breeds. This very intelligent dog guards livestock, herds pigs, and is useful in the yard, where she keeps down the rodent population. The coarse curly coat sheds and is not easy to maintain. Both breeds are extraordinarily alert and prone to barking.

Tibetan Terrier

Shoulder height: 14–16 inches for a male, females somewhat smaller

Weight: 18–30 pounds

Color: all colors except chocolate and liver brown

The small, wavy-haired dog can still be found in the Himalayas today.

The Tibetan terrier is a misleading Western term; a better fit would be Tibetan apso (apso means "abundantly hairy"). She is a typical mountain sheepdog similar to European sheepdog breeds. Her home is the three-mile-high plateau of Tibet, where her ancestors can be traced back two thousand years. While other small Tibetan breeds were kept as cherished pets, the Tibetan terrier became a worker for fellow farmers and ranchers. She survived harsh living conditions with her people, living in extreme climates. In the 1920s, physician Dr. Agnes Greig, a working doctor in India, performed a successful operation on a wealthy Tibetan woman who gave her one of these dogs as a present. She was so fascinated with this dog, she established breeding in Europe. The Tibetan terrier is lively, playful, intelligent, obedient, and incredibly adaptable. She needs close family contact. This cheerful companion loves exercise and work. She is alert but not necessarily prone to barking. The long hair is particularly hard to care for when the dog is young. She has a long life expectancy.

Cattle Dogs and Farm Dogs

Left: The Bernese mountain dog is a reliable watchdog.

Right: The Appenzell cattle dog is an agile, confident herding dog who loves to work.

Next page, bottom: The briard

› Cattle Dogs

Prior to the existence of trains and trucks, perishable meat was transported alive on its own four legs. Cattle dealers collected animals from farmers and transported them to the market: pigs, cattle, sheep, goats, horses, even geese. They often traveled hundreds of miles to big markets in growing cities. For this purpose they needed a dog that could keep the herds together; lead them safely over obstacles, such as bridges or fords; and prevent them from breaking into fields for illegal grazing and inflicting any damage when passing through villages. The cattle had to be herded unharmed and arrive in good shape. It was hard work that required strong people and strong dogs.

The herds were made up of distressed animals torn from their families and familiar surroundings. To securely herd and lead them, the dog had to earn respect from them and be able to work independently. It is clear to see the role of the hunter here; she drives the prey and keeps them all together. She runs back and forth to make sure none fall by the wayside, and she must be omnipresent. She needed endurance, agility, and powerful sprinting abilities. Only a very muscular and powerful dog would survive an often meager diet and rough handling during these journeys. The herding dog also protected the herd from two- and four-legged thieves on the way to market and when returning with the money.

These dogs were bred from original guard dogs and working pig-dogs and owned as farm dogs whose task was to protect the cattle when moving them from the pastures to the stables. If the dog was strong and reliable, the driver would take

her along with him to the market. At the market, butchers would bring their dogs along with their cattle for extra help.

> ## Farm Dogs

The farmer needed a dog to protect the farm and all living beings there as if they were her own, with no inclination to stray, to roam around, or to poach animals. The watchdog had to very quickly learn what was required of her in order to help out with the farmer's workload. The young dog learned from older dogs, got clear indications from the farmer if she was doing something wrong, and by the time she reached adulthood, she knew exactly what she was supposed to be doing. The young dog learned to respect the head of the household.

The lifestyle of the family dog today would have been completely alien to a farm dog. The dog would have been brought up on the farm right from puppyhood and lived there until the day she died. She rarely even had a glimpse of the inside of the house. Obedience exercises such as sit, stay, and walking on a leash were unnecessary. Of course, the dog learned commands but only in the context of her work, where they made sense to her. She would have led an independent life, enjoyed the friendly affection of her people, and was well fed and treated nicely but not pampered. When necessary, she would have been put on a chain or locked in a kennel. Otherwise, this dog was always free to run around but expected to follow orders.

An attention-seeking dog needing constant entertainment would have been out of place on a farm. Farm-dog breeds have preserved some of their old spirit. They are strong, dominant, not too sensitive, and are strongly territorial dogs. They have a strong sense of self-awareness, are not easily upset, and sense when a situation is serious and they need to intervene. Adults are dutiful, rarely play, are mistrustful of strangers, and rarely socialize with other dogs. As young animals, they should be given the opportunity to learn from their environment and learn to be subordinate in the family pack. Behavior varies according to selective breeding, and there are transitional forms of herding dogs where their basic ways are still evident but somewhat watered down.

Rottweiler

Shoulder height: 24–27 inches for a male, 22–25 inches for a female

Weight: 110 pounds for a male, about 92.5 pounds for a female

Color: black with reddish brown markings

The Rottweiler makes a good service dog, therapy dog, or police dog.

This breed existed in the city of Rottweil, Germany, as far back as Roman times, as herding dogs for cattle. These fearless, robust dogs were bred by butchers to herd cattle to the market. They were also used to bait bulls in Spain. The powerful, spirited Rottweiler has a springy gait and has a combination of strength, stamina, and flexibility of movement. She has nerves of steel, is extremely confident, and she has an innate distrust of strangers. However, she is cuddly and affectionate toward her family. Her love of work and her incredible courage make her a popular sports dog that can perform many versatile tasks. Rottweilers need a consistent, sensitive upbringing, and should be left in no doubt as to who is in charge; owners will need to show a firm leadership. Puppies need to learn to be subordinate early on. For the owner, this means showing consistent behavior in order to be recognized as pack leader by the dog. If the dog has been allowed to play a dominant role within her human pack, it is very difficult to correct this. As a typical herding dog, she is not an easy dog for beginners, but her daily care is straightforward.

Bouvier des Flandres

Shoulder height: 24.5–27 inches (ideal 25.5 inches) for a male, 23–25.5 inches (ideal 24.5 inches) for a female

Weight: 77–88 pounds for a male, 59.5–77 pounds for a female

Color: gray, brindle or sooty, black

Bouviers are used as guard dogs and police dogs.

This ancient herding breed and butcher's dog comes from Flanders, Belgium. The Bouvier des Flandres, also called the Vlaamse Koehond, is a shaggy, coarse-haired dog whose breeding was not regulated. He had to work under very harsh conditions. The breed standard was created in 1912, and, from this year onward, he was purebred. The Bouvier was crossbred with the Berger Picard at this time. This strong, robust, fit dog is intelligent and eager to learn but his temperament and self-confidence call for consistent, thorough training. He is an excellent watchdog and guard dog, and although not overly aggressive toward strangers, he is wary of them. Puppies must be carefully socialized and learn to be subordinate early on. He is not a dog for inexperienced owners or those who do not enjoy being active.

The Bouvier needs plenty of exercise and meaningful tasks. The coarse fur needs regular, thorough brushing and is easier to deal with when kept short.

33

Entlebuch Cattle Dog and Appenzell Cattle Dog

Entlebuch Cattle Dog
(right)

Shoulder height: 17–19.5 inches for a male, 16.5–19 inches for a female

Weight: about 45–65 pounds

Color: black with yellow to reddish brown and white markings

Appenzell Cattle Dog
(below)

Shoulder height: 20–23 inches for a male, 19–22 inches for a female

Weight: about 49–70 pounds

Color: black or Havana brown with reddish brown and white markings

Some Entlebuch cattle dogs are born with stumpy tails.

These ancient cattle dog breeds were named after their places of origin in Switzerland. At the end of the nineteenth century, a similar type of breed was known to locals, and this dog was bred according to established criteria, which stressed the differences between the Entlebuch cattle dog and the Appenzell cattle dog. By 1924, the **Entlebuch** was almost extinct. Today, this useful, low maintenance dog with the friendly yet wise facial expressions and spirited temperament has many fans, for example, people who want a working dog that is not too large. He is always attentive, learns quickly, and is willing to please. He has a fearless nature and a good watching and guarding instinct.

The **Appenzell cattle dog** is still seen working as a cattle herder today. He is lively and keen to work, wary of strangers, and more agile and demanding than the Entlebuch. These typical farm dogs are well adapted to modern life, but they cannot deny their heritage, are very confident, and tend to be dominant. An owner who can deal with this spirited dog and make it clear who is boss will find this dog to be a joyful companion, particularly in dog sports. Both breeds are very much people dogs, with robust health and easy-to-care-for coats.

Australian Cattle Dog

Shoulder height: 18–20
inches for a male, 17–19
inches for a female

Weight: about 35–45
pounds

Color: mottled blue or red

The Australian cattle dog is
also known as the blue or
red heeler.

This cattle herding dog was not replaced until very recently by motorbikes and helicopters, which are now used to herd cattle over the infinite expanse of Australia. On the farms, this breed is still indispensable; he works in the pens and helps to herd the cattle. British settlers brought collies with them to Australia. They had difficulty herding half-wild cattle in a hot, dry country, so they were crossbred with the dingo, a wild dog native to Australia, in order to produce a more resilient breed. It is thought they were later crossed with bull terriers, Dalmatians, and kelpies. The puppies are born white and gradually get their characteristic markings. This dog makes an ideal workmate on the ranch, and despite his physique, he is extremely agile. This powerful breed is always attentive, extremely intelligent, watchful, courageous, reliable, and conscientious.

He is suspicious of strangers and proves to be a loyal protector of his family. This confident dog learns quickly and needs a good master and has proved himself to be very versatile at dog sports. This family dog, so popular in Australia, is also now an established breed in the United States.

35

Bernese Mountain Dog

Shoulder height: 25–27.5 inches (ideal 26–27 inches) for a male, 23–26 inches (ideal 23.5–25 inches) for a female

Weight: about 90–120 pounds for a male, about 70–100 pounds for a female

Color: jet black with reddish brown and white markings on head, chest, and paws

To prevent damage to bones and joints, diet and exercise must be carefully monitored in young dogs.

This breed originates from Swiss cattle and farm dogs. The Bernese mountain dog owes his popularity not only to his colorful beauty but also to his lovely temperament. He is friendly and willing to work but does not need to be constantly busy. He is vigilant but not aggressive. A Bernese mountain dog loves walking; however, his desire to move is not limitless. This makes him an ideal companion dog as long as he can work as a guard dog for his people and can have regular contact with his owner. He loves to be outdoors and is not really an indoor dog. The puppies are very boisterous, and they require a consistent, loving upbringing. The Bernese cannot deny his origins or innate behavior, and he must learn very early on to be subordinate. If he is not properly trained, the males in particular will try to dominate the pack, which must be avoided as this dog is very powerful and self-aware. Once he has been well trained, he is a good companion and also an ideal tracking and disaster rescue dog. The long smooth fur is easy to care for. Unfortunately, this dog is often bred for profit so ensure you choose your breeder with care.

Great Swiss Mountain Dog

Shoulder height: 25.5–28 inches for a male, 23.6–27 inches for a female

Weight: about 105–140 pounds for a male, about 85–110 pounds for a female

Color: black with reddish brown and white markings

This breed is very territorial; males are especially intolerant.

Individual breeds began to be registered at the end of the nineteenth century in Switzerland. In 1908, the well-known canine expert Professor Albert Heim came across a short-haired Bernese mountain dog, recognized it as a breed in its own right, and named it the Great Swiss mountain dog. This impressive dog is a typical farm dog; he is not submissive by nature and must learn right from the start to be subordinate. He is therefore not a dog for beginners. If well trained, he is a balanced adult dog with a good protective instinct without being overly aggressive. He needs plenty of space and a close family connection, but he is not a dog that needs to be constantly busy and does not enjoy too much running. He enjoys spending time in the house and yard and does not tend to stray. He is hardy in all weathers and easy to care for. He is an ideal guard dog for an estate or farm. He has an excellent nose, and, as long as he acknowledges his owner as the boss, he can make a great companion dog. He is also ideal for disaster rescue and avalanche rescue training.

Russian Black Terrier

Shoulder height: 26–28 inches for a male, 25–27.5 inches for a female

Weight: 110–123 pounds for a male, 99–110 pounds for a female

Color: black or black with gray

The fur is slightly wavy, easy to maintain, and can be styled.

The Russian black terrier was developed in the former U.S.S.R. by the state as a military/working dog. They began crossbreeding the Airedale, Rottweiler, and giant schnauzers with native black schnauzer/terrier breed types. It was hoped this new breed would have the Airedale's endurance and obedience, the giant schnauzer's size and aggressiveness, and the Rottweiler's powerful physique and balanced nature. The tchiorny terrier, as it was then called, proved to be adaptable to the different climates of Russia, robust, willing to learn, and easy to train. He had nerves of steel, quick reactions, and was always ready to defend without any undesirable aggressive traits. This breed tends to have a close bond with just his owner. Therefore, he was not suitable as a service dog with multiple owners, so authorities abandoned the breeding program and breeding continued in private hands. He became known as a well-balanced companion dog and won many fans abroad as well. He needs a close family connection, attention, and should be given plenty of meaningful tasks. This sensitive dog loves to be outdoors and is not a city dog. He is suspicious of strangers but very loyal to his owner. When buying a puppy, make sure that the whole litter is good natured and has been raised with plenty of human contact.

Giant Schnauzer

Shoulder height: 23.5–27.5 inches

Weight: 77–103.5 pounds

Color: black, pepper and salt

If the dog's fur is trimmed regularly, it is easy to care for and does not shed.

The largest offspring of the schnauzer family was bred by Bavarian farmers and butchers. They called him the Russian schnauzer, the bear, or the Munich schnauzer, or to describe the large coarse-haired protector of the brewery wagon, the beer schnauzer. It is not really known which breeds were involved in creating these giants. Some say the Great Dane, the poodle, and the schnauzer. He is a spirited daredevil that can be calm and collected when required, a fearless dog with a benign character and a good protection instinct. The awe-inspiring giant has a tender heart and requires close contact with his people and a consistent leadership without undue severity; patience and understanding are required when rearing this dog. A first-class, but not entirely docile, sports dog, he is also a great family dog when one knows how to handle him. He needs work and plenty of exercise; he is not a dog that is simply happy to follow along with the family's daily life. He demands his share of attention and responsibilities and must learn from an early age to be subordinate. In 1925, the giant schnauzer was officially recognized as a service dog and is occasionally used by the police as an explosives detector and a disaster response dog. He is not an ideal dog for beginners.

Pembroke Welsh Corgi and Cardigan Welsh Corgi

Shoulder height:
Pembroke: 10–12 inches; *Cardigan:* 12 inches

Weight: *Pembroke:* 22–26.5 pounds for a male, 22–24 pounds for a female; *Cardigan:* 25–38 pounds

Color: *Pembroke:* red, sable, fawn, black and tan, with or without white markings; *Cardigan:* all colors except predominantly white

Some Pembrokes are born with stumpy tails.

Above: Pembroke Welsh corgis

Below: a Cardigan Welsh corgi

One may think of the corgi as the short-legged variant of the Welsh heeler, the Welsh herding dog. Shorter leg bones are a genetic mutation in dogs that people took advantage of and bred on purpose. Because of his short legs, he could nip at the heels of stubborn bulls to drive them as far as needed, and the dog could dart in and out of cattle hooves in a flash. He also kept down the rat and mice populations. In addition, the corgi is a vigilant watchdog and capable of chasing off an intruder. This medium-sized dog on short legs is always attentive and always on duty. He is intelligent, confident, and needs consistent training and meaningful tasks. He will challenge the ranking in his family pack, so he needs to learn to be subordinate right from puppyhood. There are two versions of this breed that were bred from the original type. The **Cardigan** is very strong and has an easygoing temperament, always has a long tail, and is available in many colors. The **Pembroke** has gone down in the history books as being the favorite breed of Queen Elizabeth II of England.

Old English Sheepdog

Shoulder height: minimum of 24 inches for a male, minimum of 22 inches for a female

Weight: about 70–90 pounds for a male, about 60–80 pounds for a female

Color: all shades of gray, blue, or blue merle with or without white markings

Congenital stumpy tails are rare. The fur can be spun to make wool.

The bobtail (stubby tail) or Old English sheepdog belongs to the shaggy-haired sheepdog breeds. After the extinction of wolves in England, this breed became a herding dog for cattle. Once she was no longer needed for this task, breeders rescued this breed from extinction. This is a powerful, robust, confident dog whose cattle herding roots cannot be denied. She must learn to be subordinate within a pack right from the start and be brought up with love and consistency. She requires a close family bond. She is vigilant without being aggressive, lively, and very intelligent but sometimes quite pigheaded. Due to her strong personality and the enormous grooming expenditure required for this dog, she must never be purchased without careful consideration. Domestic dogs need about four hours of grooming a week, and significantly more time is required in bad weather or for show dogs. This work-loving dog needs plenty to do and must be exercised in all weathers. She has a characteristic rattling bark that is said to sound like a cracked bell. She is not a dog for inactive people nor people who like to keep their homes in a pristine condition, unless they decide to have the dog's fur shorn.

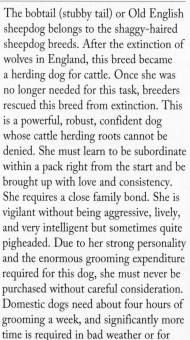

French Herding Dogs

Briard

Shoulder height: 24.5–27 inches for a male, 22–25 inches for a female

Weight: about 75–100 pounds for a male, about 50–65 pounds for a female

Color: black, gray, fawn (blonde to brown), no white markings

Beauceron

Shoulder height: 25.5–27.5 inches for a male, 24–27 inches for a female

Weight: about 65–85 pounds

Color: black and tan and harlequin (gray flecked, gray, black, tan)

Berger Picard

Shoulder height: 23.5–25.5 inches for a male, 21.5–23.5 inches for a female

Weight: about 50–70 pounds

Color: gray, gray black, gray blue, reddish gray, light or dark fawn, or a mixture of these colors

The harlequin color is a black and tan base coat with some gray mixed in, also known as merle.

These breeds herded large herds of cattle in the Northwest of France and were ideal to perform all tasks required in dealing with sheep and cattle. They also guarded the home and the farm. These dogs are very intelligent and eager to learn but only when they are taught to respect their owner and pack leader. The young dog must learn to submit to her pack leader and accept her place in the pack; if not, she will defend her role as pack leader. These dogs are very vigorous and spirited, and they are not easy to train. An owner who knows how to deal with these dogs will have a wonderful companion that gets involved in everything and needs to be a working dog, anything from agility to disaster rescue training. The **Briard** is popular due to her attractive coat, but she should never be purchased solely for her appearance. She is not a dog for

beginners. The long coat is not as easy to maintain as it once was when she was bred to be a farm dog. The young dog's fur becomes matted very easily, and the puppy needs to get used to lying

on a grooming table to have her fur groomed. This is an important part of her training and will make grooming her much easier later in life.

The **Beauceron** is a popular working dog in France. Her training must be consistent and carried out with plenty of love and empathy. She is a companion with nerves of steel, and despite her protective, confident nature, she is not a dangerous dog. However, with improper rearing and training, she can be unpredictable. In the home, she is quiet, attentive, and eager to please. She needs a task to do that fulfills her and keeps her busy.

The **Berger Picard** is very rare, despite her pleasant character. She needs a friendly yet consistent upbringing and is generally easier to train than the other two breeds. She is a true outdoor dog for active people.

Herding Dogs

Left: The Maremma sheepdog was bred in Italy. It is similar to the Great Pyrenees, Hungarian Kuvasz, and Polish Tatra.

Right: The Hungarian komondor is a typical steppe shepherd dog.

Far right: The Polish Tatra shepherd dog is a dutiful watchdog.

Bottom: The Spanish mastiff guards his territory.

Herding dogs are among the oldest companions of people. When humans no longer needed to hunt their prey but began to breed animals and keep them under their care so that they could have access to essential items such as milk, meat, fur, and wool, they had to protect these animals from predators and thieves. Without dogs, humans could not have accomplished this important step in their cultural development. When the wolf was largely eradicated in Europe, overly large, strong dogs were no longer needed. Some remained as guard dogs in the home. These very large dogs have remained as herding dogs in only the most remote mountainous regions of Europe where wolves and bears still live.

In the wake of dog breeding at the end of the nineteenth century, some ancient breeds were rescued from extinction and purebred for other purposes. In the late twentieth century, the wolf population rose and the herding dog once again became more important for protection against these predators.

The herding dog is still deeply rooted in tradition; some were bred as companion dogs in recent decades, and they adapted to people's needs. Nevertheless, her essential characteristics still remain even if they are not immediately obvious. Most pronounced are the territorial instinct, hunting instinct, and herding instinct; the sexual instinct also plays a minor role. The herding dog guards the herds while her master sleeps. She grows up with the flock and regards them as her property, which she will defend and never leave. Her master feeds her, so she does not help herself to the livestock. She awaits orders from her owner but is able to work independently. The shepherd treasures the dog and her work. She is self-sufficient and the dominance of humans is never in question. In some cases, the dog lives with the sheep; the shepherd only comes over once a day, milks the

is often irrelevant. The sovereign dog decides when her intervention with real or perceived threats is necessary and has lightning-quick reactions. That makes her unpredictable to the layperson. She

sheep, tends to them, and feeds the dog. In other circumstances, the shepherd remains constantly with his herds and has a closer relationship with his dog.

The herding dog has an important duty to perform; she has to grow up and carry responsibilities. So her time as a new puppy with games and fun is soon over for her. Whatever she did not learn as a puppy she will not learn as an adult. The big, strong, fast-reacting dog may then be uncontrollable and willing to enforce her position in the pack with her teeth, if necessary. She is calm and introverted in the daytime and attentive as night falls. She is very reluctant to leave her territory, is mistrustful of strangers, and will defend her property against intruders. She will not tolerate strange dogs within her vast territory and will regularly scent-mark the area. In this context, gender

is very uncertain when in an unfamiliar territory; she knows that she has nothing to lose and nothing to defend. Herding dogs are true outdoor dogs and love the outdoor life; they will protect anything humans entrust to them. Owners need a good, sound knowledge of herding dog characteristics, a natural authority when dealing with dogs, a good knowledge of canine behavior in general, and a large, secured area to keep the dog in. Females are usually significantly more cooperative than males. The dog is not suited to cramped living conditions in the city or sports activities. She is suited for people who like having a dog around them at all times, but she does not need constant entertainment from her owner.

Hovawart

Shoulder height: 25–27.5 inches for a male, 23–25.5 inches for a female

Weight: about 77–99 pounds for a male, about 62–77 pounds for a female

Color: black and tan, black, and blond

The slightly wavy long fur with a fine undercoat is easy to maintain.

In medieval literature, the Hovawart, "farm watchman" in old German, is depicted as a long-haired, floppy-eared, large, extremely strong dog. German zoologist Kurt F. König was inspired by the breed, and at the beginning of the twentieth century, he crossed farm dogs from the Harz and Odenwald mountain ranges with sheep and mountain dogs, Newfoundlands, shaggy-haired sheepdogs, and other breeds of unknown origin. In 1922, the first litter of Hovawarts was registered and the breed was officially recognized in 1937. The Hovawart has been a well-known service dog since 1964.

Hovawarts still have a high amount of sheepdog and farm-dog blood in them; they exhibit territorial behavior and are not submissive. Many years of selective breeding made this dog an excellent sports and service dog due to his strength and tenacity. Hovawarts need a lot of exercise and meaningful tasks and are not suitable for people with an inactive lifestyle or those who live in the city. A good knowledge of canine behavior is needed in order to ensure this confident dog retains a subordinate position in the pack. This requires experience and consistency. If successful, the owner will have a hardworking, delightful dog that loves sports and can also undertake serious tasks such as disaster and avalanche rescue training. This dog is a happy, lovable companion that needs close contact with his people.

Leonberger

Shoulder height: 28–31.5 inches (ideal 30 inches) for a male, 25.5–29.5 inches (ideal 27.5 inches) for a female

Weight: about 120–170 pounds for a male, about 100–135 pounds for a female

Color: lion yellow, gold to reddish brown, sandy colors with black mask

The long, sleek fur with a dense undercoat is easy to maintain and does not hide the contours of his fine physique.

When pedigree dog breeding first began, it was not only indigenous breeds that were furthered; new breeds were bred by enthusiasts. Heinrich Essig, town councilman of Leonberg, Germany, was a professional dog breeder and dog handler and was very influential in dog breeding at the time. The Leonberger was ostensibly bred as a "symbolic dog" that would mimic the lion in the town crest. Breeds that contributed to this new breed were the Landseer, Saint Bernard, and Great Pyrenees mountain dog. The first Leonberger was born in 1846. Essig knew how to market his new breed and Empress Elisabeth of Austria, Napoleon III, and the Prince of Wales were counted as his customers, among others. The Leonberger still exhibits typical herding behaviors today. He herds peacefully and loyally protects his family and property. He treasures his walks and patrols his territory, but he is not a great lover of running and will not tolerate any other dogs in the area he regards as his territory. He must be well socialized and trained from an early age so that he learns to be subordinate. Owners need a good knowledge of canine behavior and a natural air of authority to ensure the dog knows his place in the pack. However, severe, overly strict training will achieve nothing. The owner must consistently prove his leadership abilities in order to rear a pleasant family dog. The rearing of the young dog requires great care so he does not grow too fast and overburden the bones and joints. Unfortunately, the Leonberger does not have a high life expectancy. The average lifespan is about seven years.

Saint Bernard

Shoulder height: 27.5–35.5 inches for a male, 25.5–31.5 inches for a female

Weight: 130–180 pounds

Color: white with reddish brown patches or mantle (back and flanks)

Coat: long-haired and short-haired varieties

Long-haired and short-haired Saint Bernard coats are both easy to maintain.

Above: long-haired coat

Below: short-haired coat

Since the eighteenth century, the Saint Bernard has helped guides on the mountains to locate missing travelers, assisting them along the paths through fog and darkness. The legendary Barry, a rescue dog that worked for the Great Saint Bernard Hospice in Switzerland in the early eighteen hundreds, is reported to have rescued forty people during his lifetime. The breed originated from red and white farm dogs. They were strong, short-haired, light in comparison to today's Saint Bernards, and could move well in heavy snow. Long-haired puppies stayed with the farmers in the valley where they attracted the interest of affluent British tourists. Tales of the heroic Barry made the breed became very fashionable in England, where it was bred with Newfoundlands and mastiffs to make it the giant breed well known today. The Saint Bernard is no longer intended for work in the snow. He does not have much need for running, but he does require regular exercise. He does not display typical sheep or farm-dog properties and is not as infinitely good natured as his reputation promises. He must learn early on to be subordinate, needs clear leadership, and he will defend his territory. Today breeding trends lean toward a more mobile and lighter build, and the eyelids and lips can now close. Unfortunately, he does not have a high life expectancy. His lifespan is about eight to ten years.

Caucasian Shepherd, Tibetan Mastiff, Anatolian Shepherd

Caucasian Shepherd
Shoulder height: minimum 25.5 inches for a male, minimum 24.5 inches for a female

Weight: minimum 110 pounds for a male, minimum 99 pounds for a female

Color: white, brown, spotted, or mottled

Tibetan Mastiff
Shoulder height: minimum 26 inches for a male, minimum 24 inches for a female

Weight: 141–172 pounds

Color: black, black gray, blue with or without tan, golden

Anatolian Shepherd
Shoulder height: 29–32 inches for a male, 28–31 inches for a female

Weight: 110–143 pounds for a male, 88–121 pounds for a female

Color: all allowed

These ancient shepherd dog breeds fell into the hands of American pedigree dog breeders just a few generations ago, with the possible exception of the **Tibetan mastiff**, also called the Do Khyi. **Caucasian shepherds** were kept in Soviet times as vigilant guard dogs by the military with harsh boundaries and were seen as a particularly difficult breed, as was the Kangal, officially known as the **Anatolian shepherd**. Unfortunately, their reputation attracted owners who were unsuitable for this type of dog. The difficulties of these dog breeds are popular topics of discussion among canine behavioral experts!

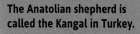
The Anatolian shepherd is called the Kangal in Turkey.

Above: a Caucasian shepherd from Russia

Left: a Tibetan mastiff

Right: an Anatolian shepherd

Slovakian Chuvach, Polish Tatra Shepherd, Great Pyrenees, Pyrenean Mastiff

Slovakian Chuvach

(bottom left)

Shoulder height: 24.5–27.5 inches for a male, 23–25.5 inches for a female

Weight: 79–97 pounds for a male, 68–81.5 pounds for a female

Color: white

Polish Tatra Shepherd

(center)

Shoulder height: 25.5–27.5 inches for a male, 23.5–25.5 inches for a female

Weight: 110–130 pounds for a male, 90–110 pounds for a female

Color: white

Great Pyrenees (from France) (top)

Shoulder height: 27.5–31.5 inches for a male, 25.5–29.5 inches for a female

Weight: 115 pounds for a male, 85–90 pounds for a female

Color: white or white with gray or orange spots on the ears

Pyrenean Mastiff (from Spain) (bottom right)

Shoulder height: minimum 30 inches (ideally at least 32 inches) for a male, minimum 28 inches (ideally at least 29.5 inches) for a female

Weight: 179–220 pounds

Color: white with colored markings

These dogs shed a lot.

These white shepherd breeds are closely related. The pure white color appeared in some of the earlier breeds. For generations they have been bred as service dogs and have adapted well to life with humans. With correct rearing and training, which must be shown consistently to puppies, they can make good family pets. Nevertheless, they are typical sheepdogs; they need their own space to guard and need strong leadership. With good care, the coat stays white and does not need to be washed.

Kuvasz

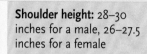

Shoulder height: 28–30 inches for a male, 26–27.5 inches for a female

Weight: 106–136.5 pounds for a male, 81.5–110 pounds for a female

Color: white, ivory also permitted

The excessively coarse, wavy fur rarely becomes matted but sheds a lot during the change of coat.

The Kuvasz originated from pastoral tribes in Asia who traveled to the area known today as Hungary. In the Middle Ages, the beautiful white dog was the hound of choice for royalty. During the world wars, the breed suffered serious setbacks, and in 1956, during the Hungarian Revolution, the breed almost reached extinction. If these brave dogs prevented soldiers from entering their territory, they would be shot at close range. Fortunately, this beautiful white dog had many fans in Europe and the United States, which enabled the breed to recover. The Kuvasz is one of the most famous all–white sheepdogs and has been an established breed for many years. The incredibly beautiful dog has a strong personality and marked sense of hierarchy. Consistent training must begin from puppyhood. The fast–growing, vigorous, and very spirited dog demands patience and perseverance from his owner. Once he has found his place in the family and accepted his owner as the boss, the Kuvasz is a pleasant, adaptable housemate and a reliable guard dog. The breeding standard emphasizes that if this dog is poorly treated he is likely to become aggressive. The Kuvasz needs adequate space for exercise as an outlet for his energy; however, his hunting instinct can be repressed by consistent training.

51

Newfoundland

Shoulder height: average 28 inches for a male, average 26 inches for a female

Weight: 150 pounds for a male, 119 pounds for a female

Color: black, brown, white with black markings

The oily, dense, waterproof short-haired coat is difficult to care for.

Newfoundlands were descendants of European sheepdogs, which the fishermen used as guard dogs on the coast of Newfoundland in Canada. English fishermen discovered this breed in Newfoundland and took them home. Initially, they were large black and white dogs, but they were also crossed with the smaller black dog breeds from the south island of St. Johns. This bear-like dog superseded the Landseer as the dog of choice for wealthy Brits. His passion for water and an innate love of retrieving make the Newfoundland a born water rescue dog.

The most famous person to be saved by one of these dogs was Napoleon, who was rescued by the legendary Boatswain. As a water rescue dog, aggression and guarding instincts were not necessary or desirable. The spirited young dog must be brought up with strict training; otherwise, he will try to dominate. A Newfoundland needs plenty of space, loves to be outdoors, and needs close family contact. However, he is content with short walks. He is quick to learn but too heavy for dog sports and also not willing to be subordinate enough. He is unsuitable as an apartment dog or a city dog.

Landseer

Shoulder height: 28–31.5 inches for a male, 26–28 inches for a female

Weight: 143–176 pounds for a male, 110–154 pounds for a female

Color: white with black head and flanks

The Landseer makes a good water rescue dog.

Portuguese and Basque fishermen took herding dog breeds with them to the coast of Newfoundland for the protection of ships and settlers. The dogs helped haul in the nets, brought castaways to land, pulled in boats and other equipment out of the water, and dragged nets of wood from the forest while attached to a harness. These robust, powerful animals survived under extremely harsh conditions. In the eighteenth century, fishermen brought the first Landseer dogs to England, where the powerful yet friendly dog won many fans. The Landseer was named after the famous artist Sir Edwin Landseer, who depicted these dogs with landed gentry in numerous paintings. This breed still has sheepdog traits, but his protective instinct and aggression are no longer needed because crews were constantly changing, and aggressive dogs were not useful or welcome. He is convincingly threatening, loyal to his territory, and will defend it if necessary. He is a confident dog that needs to be trained consistently from an early age and should be assigned a lower ranking in the pack. Because his overall mood is not generally aggressive, he tends to use stubbornness or exuberance rather than his teeth to express himself. He loves to be outdoors and enjoys walks but does not really feel the need to run. He needs his own living space to guard and a close bond with his family. He is quick and eager to learn and loves to work.

53

Gundogs With Handlers

Left: The pointer suddenly freezes and points the tip of her nose in the direction of her prey.

Right: Springer spaniels love to forage.

Bottom: The large Münsterländer is very versatile.

"Gundogs with handlers" are breeds that work in a team with the hunter as pack leader to ensure the success of the hunt. Because of this, these breeds differ substantially from gundogs without handlers. They do not hunt in a chaotic group, but rather in a well-organized pack with assigned roles and a pack leader to whom the dogs are subordinate. For dog owners, this means a dog that is intelligent, willing to please, and eager to learn. The rest of the pack organize the roles among themselves and obey the pack leader. However, as a professional hunting dog, her passion for hunting is at the forefront of her mind. The owner needs to ensure the skills of this dog are honed so that she obeys her master and also the gunshot. This means the owner must take on the role of providing the loot and killing the prey; this shows the dog that the owner is a good leader because he hunts and shares the spoils with the pack.

Those who do not hunt with their gundog will find it difficult to prove who is in charge. Conventional training with senseless commands will not get you very far. Gundogs, with the exception of a few, are therefore unsuitable as family dogs. They will use every opportunity to follow their innate tendencies and can hardly take their owner seriously if he does not hunt with the dog, let alone be subordinate to him. This results in a very unsatisfactory situation for both dog and owner!

› Pointing Breeds

The pointer searches in an open field with great speed and tireless stamina. If she finds a scent, she displays classic pointer behavior—stopping still and pointing her nose in the direction of her prey. The hunter gives the command to continue walking slowly and calmly until the birds take off or the hare starts to run, and then the hunter can shoot.

Because this book is primarily aimed at dog fans who do not hunt, technical hunting terms have not been used; we have used layman's terms instead.

The dog is not allowed to run after the game but must stay where she is, either lying down or sitting for her own safety. In areas where birds and other game can hide in longer vegetation,

bushes or reeds, edges of the forest, rivers, and hedges, a hunter will need the smaller type of flushing dog that forages through the designated area and tracks the wildlife, keeping the hunter in her sight. The dog must work independently; however, she remains in communication with the hunter by barking consistently along the scent track, and she must immediately be called back if she is hunting the game in the wrong direction. This type of dog works with the hunter in a team, retrieves the prey, and brings it back to her "pack leader."

> Retrievers

Retrievers are trained to wait patiently behind the hunter for the command to race across the field to retrieve the game. Waterfowl is a popular type of game; for this, a hunter requires a dog that loves to be in the water and is happy to jump straight in, even in freezing temperatures. This is the work of the retriever. Because they do not hunt independently and are willing to please—in other words, they work on command—this makes them a good companion dog for the family.

> All-Around Gundogs

These gundogs have the full spectrum of hunting skills: following a scent, flushing, foraging, then retrieving. They are incredibly tough, persistent, passionate, and lively, but not exactly willing to be subordinate and need very consistent training. German pointers have consistently proven to be one of the best all-around gundogs. Some have a very pronounced protective instinct because they are trained to attack when being pursued by poachers. This breed is known as the police dog of the forest.

> Transitional Gundogs With and Without Handlers

Here we find the descendants of the ancient hounds that adapted to our hunting conditions; a dog that does not submit to her pack leader has no place here. These dogs are very versatile with the exception of bloodhounds.

Setters

Irish Red Setter
Shoulder height: 23–26 inches for a male, 21.5–24.5 inches for a female

Weight: 60–70 pounds

Color: rich chestnut brown with no traces of black

English Setter
Shoulder height: 25.5–27 inches for a male, 24–25.5 inches for a female

Weight: 60–65 pounds for a male, 50–55 pounds for a female

Color: the flecking on the coat is called belton: white with black spots (blue belton), white with orange spots, white with lemon spots, or white liver brown spots; blue belton or liver belton with tan (tricolored)

Gordon Setter
Shoulder height: 26 inches for a male, 24.5 inches for a female

Weight: 65 pounds for a male, 56 pounds for a female

Color: black with rich chestnut

Top: an Irish setter

Next page, top: an English setter

Next page, bottom left: a Gordon setter

Next page, bottom right: an Irish red and white setter

Setters are independent working dogs with great endurance. They are clever and quick to learn, but they need clear leadership to learn to be obedient. Someone with good knowledge of canine behavior will find it easier to train a setter. They are suitable as family dogs as long as you find a way to keep them busy according to their natural inclinations. Simply exercising them, going for a bike ride with your setter running by your side, for example, is not enough. They love to hunt, but at the same time, they are very pleasant family dogs. Such tasks as disaster rescue training, involving searching among rubble, are ideal for this breed. In general, setters tend to be very underutilized and are difficult to keep busy. Unfortunately, they are often purchased for their beauty without any regard to their innate needs, hunting in particular. In this case, it is better to find a family dog with a less pronounced passion for hunting.

English Setter

In the nineteenth century, Sir Edward Laverack crossed a spaniel with a pointer. The resulting breed, the English setter, specializes in searching vast areas during the hunt. Calm in the house, her lively spirit is unleashed when outdoors. The temperament of the English setter lies somewhere between the Irish setter and the Gordon setter. She is not for people with an inactive lifestyle.

Gordon Setter

In the eighteenth century, the Duke of Gordon bred a more powerful, less elegant dog to work on the difficult terrain of Scotland. The Gordon setter is

Irish Red and White Setter

Shoulder height: 24.5–26 inches for a male, 22.5–24 inches for a female

Weight: 50–75 pounds

Color: white with reddish-brown flecks

The silky, smooth fur (wavy in the case of the English setter) has no undercoat but requires regular grooming.

a one-person dog that is reserved toward strangers and does not cope well with a change of owner. She takes a long time to mature and needs consistent training right from the very start.

Irish Red Setter

The Irish red setter enjoys great international popularity. She searches vast areas and is a faster and more persistent pointer. She is suitable for water work, an efficient hunter and retriever, and is particularly good at chasing away poachers. This lively breed, always on the lookout for wildlife, has a distinctive love of hunting. This dog requires an owner who enjoys sport and who can spend plenty of time with his dog and train her sensitively—not an easy task for a dog as spirited and confident as this breed.

Irish Red and White Setter

This is the oldest type of Irish setter. She is powerful and more athletic than the Irish red setter, friendly, intelligent, and eager to work. She is also a passionate hunting dog though not quite as lively as the Irish red.

57

Pointer

Shoulder height: 25–27 inches for a male, 24–26 inches for a female

Weight: 44–75 pounds

Color: lemon and white, orange and white, liver and white, and black and white; also solid colors or tricolors

It is bred as either a show dog or gundog; they have different physiques.

The pointer is the classic setter whose ancestors are from both the Iberian Peninsula and England. England is famous for breeding dogs that are specialized in every area of hunting. Hunting events can be found for every gundog breed and there are always sporting competitions or field trials in every county in England. This noble, quick, purebred hound was the starting point of all German pointer breeds, as well as many other breeds. She runs at breakneck speed with inexhaustible perseverance, and, as her name implies, she points her nose toward the game. The more birds she finds, the better. The pointer is a very fast, tenacious, and vivacious dog that is rarely suited to life as a family dog, despite the fact that she does have a very amiable character and is easy to care for. Her innate need for running and her passion for hunting are suited to a person who goes hunting on a regular basis.

Springer Spaniels

English Springer Spaniel
Shoulder height: approximately 20 inches

Weight: 40–50 pounds

Color: liver and white, black and white, or either of these colors with tan markings

Welsh Springer Spaniel
Shoulder height: 19 inches for a male, 18 inches for a female

Weight: 35–50 pounds

Color: red and white only

Careful skin and ear care is required, though this care is less time consuming than for the cocker spaniel.

English Springer Spaniel

This breed is one of the most popular breeds of all time in England and was originally bred from the Rochester spaniel, which can be traced back six hundred years. Back then, she drove the birds into the nets. Today the springer is an excellent gundog that forages extensively to flush out the wildlife and then retrieve it. She is very fond of water. She is a friendly, affectionate, reliable dog that needs plenty of meaningful tasks. She is ideal for the lone hunter but has also proved to be a very pleasant family dog. She is suitable as a family pet as long as she is trained consistently and is given plenty to do. If underutilized, she will indulge in her passion for hunting anyway.

Top: an English springer spaniel
Right: a Welsh springer spaniel

Welsh Springer Spaniel

This very tough, tenacious dog is well adapted to the Welsh terrain and has many good hunting qualities. She is also a pleasant family dog, easy to train, and very spirited. You will need to give her meaningful tasks; she is not suitable for people with an inactive lifestyle.

English Cocker Spaniel and American Cocker Spaniel

English Cocker Spaniel

Shoulder height: 15–16 inches for a male, 15 inches for a female

Weight: 27.5–32 pounds

Color: *solid:* red, black, golden, liver, black and tan, liver and tan; *bicolor:* black and white, orange and white, liver and white, lemon and white; *tricolor:* black, white, and tan or liver, white, and tan; *roan:* blue roan, orange roan, lemon roan, liver roan, blue roan and tan, liver roan and tan

American Cocker Spaniel

Shoulder height: ideal: 15 inches for a male, 14 inches for a female

Weight: 24–28 pounds

Color: *solid:* black, black with tan points, cream to dark red and brown with or without tan markings; *multicolored:* black and white, red and white, brown and white, and roan, any of these with or without tan markings

Both breeds require regular skin and ear care.

English Cocker Spaniel

This breed originates from Spanish bird dogs and was bred in England to hunt woodcocks. He is an excellent flushing dog that loves to retrieve as well as track. He is very intelligent, affectionate, and cuddly, while spirited, always happy, playful, and ever ready for walks. His excellent nose, love of work, and his playfulness make him ideal for tracking drugs, explosives, and other such things. This charming dog, with his innocent facial expressions, needs plenty of training because he knows very well how to wrap his owner around his little paw. He has an enormous appetite and is always hungry. This gundog must be kept busy; otherwise, he will use every opportunity to forage for prey.

Top: an English cocker spaniel

Left: an American cocker spaniel

American Cocker Spaniel

In the United States, a smaller, cuter dog was bred from the English cocker spaniel and became very popular as a family dog. As a show breed, his fur was overemphasized and is now a handicap; it requires a lot of care, which makes many people now think twice about owning this dog. He is an affectionate, happy family dog, gentle and easy to train. He is very sensitive to the needs of his humans, likes to be in close contact, and is always alert but not noisy. His prey drive can be kept under control with good training.

German Spaniel

Shoulder height: 19–21 inches for a male, 18–20.5 inches for a female

Weight: 39.5–55 pounds

Color: solid brown or red, often with white or gray markings on chest and toes; brown or red roan

The smooth, slightly wavy or curly coat is easy to care for.

One of the oldest gundogs, he was bred for flushing, and originally flushed out birds of prey during a hunt. His ancestors were hound dogs, and he himself is the precursor of the pointer. In 1897, professional German hunters began to breed these medium-sized, long-haired working dogs. The German spaniel, also known as the German Wachtelhund, is comparable with the English hunting spaniels and is therefore called the German spaniel in English-speaking countries. This spaniel is particularly suited to forest areas. He specializes in hunting and flushing on difficult terrain but is not suitable as a guard dog. He has a fine nose, is a reliable tracker, flushes with great enthusiasm for wildlife, fights off poachers, loves the water, and is an excellent retriever. He is also suitable for tracking animals that have been shot.

This pleasant hunting companion should belong only to a hunter so he can make the most of his skills. He is not really suitable for owners who can only go hunting at weekends or those who just want a family dog. Both types (dark brown and light brown with gray) are from different bloodlines and should not be bred together. The German spaniel was exclusively bred as a versatile flushing gundog by hunters for hunters.

Labrador Retriever

Shoulder height: 22–22.5 inches for a male, 21–22 inches for a female

Weight: 55–75 pounds

Color: black, yellow, liver, or chocolate brown

The dense, water-repellent coat is easy to care for but sheds profusely.

The former St. John's dog originates from southern Newfoundland. Cod fishermen brought the dogs to England in the nineteenth century and enthused over their ability to retrieve from the water. The Earl of Malmesbury bought some of these dogs and took them to his home in Labrador on the Canadian coast. They were soon famous for being excellent retrievers. Their versatility is remarkable.

The Labrador retriever is a first-class gundog for retrieving prey, excellent sniffer dog, mine detection dog, rescue dog, avalanche dog, guide dog, and family dog. He is affectionate, cuddly, and will not stray. He is a vigilant watchdog but never aggressive toward humans and animals, which makes him unsuitable as a guard dog. He has steady nerves, a balanced temperament, and is very confident. The strong, often demanding dog must be trained from an early age so that he learns to be subordinate. He needs plenty of exercise and meaningful tasks. He loves the water and will swim in both summer and winter. The Labrador has been marketed as a fashionable breed; however, he is not an easy dog due to his insatiable need for attention. Show lines have a more solid build whereas dogs from working lines tend to be slimmer.

Golden Retriever

Shoulder height: 22–24 inches for a male, 20–22 inches for a female

Weight: 55–75 pounds

Color: gold or cream, no red

The golden retriever has a "soft muzzle": when retrieving, he holds the prey gently in his mouth without injuring it.

At the end of the nineteenth century, Lord Tweedmouth in Scotland bred a yellow Labrador retriever, Irish setter, and the now-extinct Tweed water spaniel to create a retriever dog with a soft muzzle. This calm, relaxed yet attentive dog is intelligent and eager to learn. Other than gundog training, he is also used as a guide dog and responds well to obedience training and equestrian sport. The golden retriever should never be aggressive. He is not a guard dog. He needs to be trained lovingly and will give an inexperienced owner little difficulty. Because he is not the most keen hunting dog, he will not stray or kill game as long as you keep him busy. A great sport designed for retrievers is called "dummy work," where he is trained to retrieve an artificial rabbit. Unfortunately, the golden retriever is seen as a fashionable dog with all the negative consequences, such as uncontrolled mass breeding. Therefore, when buying a puppy, take great care to avoid selecting a dog with health problems and any undesirable character traits. The medium-long, sleek fur needs regular brushing.

Retrievers

Flat-Coated Retriever
(right)
Shoulder height: 23–24 inches for a male, 22–23 inches for a female
Weight: 59.5–79 pounds for a male, 55–70.5 pounds for a female
Color: black and liver brown

Chesapeake Bay Retriever
(bottom right)
Shoulder height: 23–26 inches for a male, 21–24 inches for a female
Weight: 65–80.5 pounds for a male, 55–70.5 pounds for a female
Color: all shades of brown, reddish yellow to chestnut, and a dull straw color

Nova Scotia Duck Tolling Retriever
(bottom left)
Shoulder height: 19–20 inches for a male, 18–19 inches for a female
Weight: 44–51 pounds for a male, 37.5–44 pounds for a female
Color: red orange tones with white markings on the head, chest, feet, and tail

All three breeds particularly love water work. Tolling means luring game close enough to shoot.

Flat-Coated Retriever

This retriever breed was bred at the end of the nineteenth century in England. He is docile and sensitive, not a markedly protective dog but watchful all the same. This spirited dog needs exercise and meaningful tasks. He is suitable for all dog sports and activities but is not suitable as a guard dog. His smooth coat is easy to care for. He is also ideal for inexperienced dog owners.

Chesapeake Bay Retriever

In 1807, an English ship became stranded on the coast of Maryland. On board were two Newfoundland dogs, which were then crossed with native gundogs. The resulting breed is an excellent flushing dog that will retrieve from icy water. He is lively, courageous, with nerves of steel, and needs a close family bond and plenty of meaningful tasks. He requires consistent training.

Nova Scotia Duck Tolling Retriever

This breed comes from Nova Scotia in Canada. Nova Scotia duck tolling retrievers wait on the shore until they spot a duck and then hide out of sight so they can take it by surprise. Settlers took advantage of their unusual hunting methods and bred a lively, playful, easily trainable dog that does not tend to stray.

German Short-Haired Pointing Dog and Weimaraner

German Short-Haired Pointing Dog (left)

Shoulder height: 24.5–26 inches for a male, 23–25 inches for a female

Weight: 55–70 pounds for a male, 45–60 pounds for a female

Color: brown or black, mottled white or roan

Weimaraner (bottom)

Shoulder height: 23–27.5 inches for a male, 22.5–25.5 inches for a female

Weight: 66–88 pounds for a male, 55–77 pounds for a female

Color: silver, roe, or mouse gray

This breed is aggressive and will bite on command.

German Short-Haired Pointing Dog

The German short-haired pointing dog is one of the most popular gundog breeds both in Germany and abroad. This breed originates from the Italian pointer. He was crossed with the English pointer to create a more noble short-haired breed with a lively spirit, excellent scenting capabilities, and an elegant appearance. The outspoken, versatile, often nervy dog should belong only to a hunter so he can receive appropriate training and make the most of his natural abilities. He is not suitable as a "weekend-only" gundog.

Weimaraner

Grand Duke Carl August of Weimar (1757–1828) bred this versatile, tenacious hunter in the early nineteenth century. This dog's aggressiveness is particularly pronounced. This breed is only suitable for the hunter so he can receive appropriate training and make the most of his natural abilities. He is not a docile dog and needs thorough training. Unfortunately, this unusually beautiful dog has been marketed as a family dog, but he is highly unsuitable as such. He is also a popular show dog. The long-haired Weimaraner is very rare.

65

German Wirehaired Pointer and German Rough-Haired Pointing Dog

German Wirehaired Pointer

Shoulder height: 24–27 inches for a male, 22.5–25 inches for a female

Weight: 45–75 pounds

Color: solid brown, brown with or without a white chest patch, brown roan with or without patches, black roan with or without patches, light roan

German Rough-Haired Pointing Dog

Shoulder height: 23.5–27.5 inches for a male, 23–27 inches for a female

Weight: 44 pounds

Color: solid brown, brown with a white chest patch, brown roan with or without brown patches, light roan with or without brown patches

Hunters required an aggressive dog for personal protection against poachers.

Top: a German wirehaired pointer

Right: a German rough-haired pointing dog

German Wirehaired Pointer

This breed is the most popular gundog in Germany. Although classified as a pointer breed, he is an all-arounder. He was the result of crossings with various coarse-haired pointer breeds, where strength was the only breeding objective. It soon became clear that this simple German wirehaired pointer would dominate the gundog scene. This passionate, spirited dog has nerves of steel. He is suitable for rough terrain as well as for water work. He is a tough, powerful dog that can also be aggressive. He is not docile and needs thorough gundog training. He should be owned by a hunter so he can pursue his main passion with consistent leadership. He is not a "weekend-only" gundog. The coarse coat is easy to care for.

German Rough-Haired Pointing Dog

These dogs were used in sixteenth-century Ridinger, Germany, by woodcutters; this breed is versatile, working equally well in the field, forest, and water. This water-loving dog has a predisposition to aggressive behavior. He is bred mainly in East Frisia, a region in Northern Germany. He must live life purely as a gundog.

Both breeds are real all-arounders for work in German coalfields. They belong exclusively to hunters.

Pudelpointer and Wirehaired Pointing Griffon

Pudelpointer

Shoulder height: 23.5–27 inches for a male, 21.6–25 inches for a female

Weight: 44–66 pounds

Color: dark brown, liver brown, or black

Wirehaired Pointing Griffon

Shoulder height: 21.5–23.5 inches for a male, 19.5–21.5 inches for a female

Weight: 50–60 pounds

Color: steel gray with brown patches, solid brown, brown roan, white and brown, white and orange

Pudelpointer

As the name suggests, this is a cross between a poodle and a pointer and was bred to unite the good qualities of both breeds. The first result of this breeding was a dog called Juno that resulted from a random mating between a brown male poodle and a brown female pointer. This dog excelled at his duties and was smart and personable. The poodle provided the intelligence and willingness to please, and the pointer provided a love of water, endurance, speed, and passion for hunting. The pudelpointer is characterized by his love of water, his ability to learn, enjoyment for retrieving, blood tracking, and his strength. The coat should not be of a woolly consistency and in this case is easy to maintain.

Wirehaired Pointing Griffon

In 1850, Dutchman Eduard Karel Korthals bred these water-loving, scent-tracking dogs from the French griffon in Germany. This dog is affectionate and docile with all the typical characteristics of a French pointer.

Blood tracking refers to following the trail of blood after the hunter has shot the game.

Top: a Pudelpointer

Left: a wirehaired pointing griffon

German Long-Haired Pointing Dog and Large Münsterländer

German Long-Haired Pointing Dog

Shoulder height: 23.5–27.5 inches for a male, 23–26 inches for a female

Weight: about 66 pounds

Color: solid brown, brown and white, brown with white speckles, dark roan, light roan, mottled

Large Münsterländer

Shoulder height: 23.5–25.5 inches for a male, 23–25 inches for a female

Weight: about 66 pounds

Color: white with black patches or spots, blue roan

The large Münsterländer was brought to North America in 1966.

German Long-Haired Pointing Dog

The long-haired gundog tracks the blood of birds, hawks, and waterfowl and is a very versatile hunter. In 1897, Baron von Schorlemer presented the first breed characteristics for the German long-haired pointing dog and laid the foundation for today's pedigrees. Emphasis is placed on water work and blood tracking. He is willing to please and has a calm, even temperament.

Large Münsterländer

It was originally a color variant of the German long-haired pointing dog but became a breed in its own right in 1908. The black and white variants found on farms in the Münster region of Germany had always been popular. Breeders kept this breed going because it was highly suitable for hunting both before and after shooting in areas with brambles, heather, and bogs. He was always kept as part of a family so therefore enjoys a close bond with his people and is docile, intelligent, and alert.

Kleiner Münsterländer

Kleiner Münsterländer

Shoulder height: 20.5–22 inches for a male, 19.6–21 inches for a female

Weight: about 66 pounds

Color: brown-white, brown roan with brown patches, tan markings allowed

The Kleiner Münsterländer is a docile dog that learns easily to be subordinate.

Kleiner Münsterländer

The smallest German pointer was not only a hunting companion, but also a domestic watchdog for Münsterländer farmers. He is vigilant and lively with a very affectionate nature. The generally docile dog is popular with recreational hunters but will only be content if he is able to pursue his passion for hunting. Unfortunately, he is marketed as a family dog, which is bad for both dog and owner.

Previous page, top: a German long-haired pointing dog

Previous page, bottom: a large Münsterländer

Right: a Kleiner Münsterländer

Spaniels

Brittany Spaniel (right)

Shoulder height: 19–20 inches for a male, 18.5–19.5 female

Weight: 30–40 pounds

Color: white with orange, white with brown, white with black, and tricolor

French Spaniel (bottom)

Shoulder height: 22–24 inches for a male, 22–23 inches for a female

Weight: 45–60 pounds

Color: white and brown spotted

The Brittany spaniel is a popular family dog in France.

Brittany Spaniel

The origins of the smallest French pointer, the Breton pointer or Brittany spaniel, can be traced back to the medieval bird dogs. He is popular in his homeland due to his excellent gundog skills on difficult terrain. He has a fine nose, reliably pointing to and retrieving animals shot by the hunter. He loves water work. As a classic pointer, he does not flush. He is very docile, intelligent, gentle, and sensitive. Due to his small size, he is ideal for recreational hunters and makes a great family pet.

French Spaniel

He is the oldest and most primitive French long-haired breed, the legendary dog of the Middle Ages. Like so many French breeds, he disappeared after the revolution in 1790 and made a comeback around 1850. Calm and balanced, he has proven himself as an all-around hunting dog, especially on difficult terrain, such as thickets and swamps. He enjoys working in the water and loves to retrieve.
He is very willing to please and to be subordinate. He is an intelligent dog who keeps in close contact with the hunter. He makes a good family dog as long as he is allowed to use his hunting skills.

Rhodesian Ridgeback

Shoulder height: 25–27 inches for a male, 24–26 inches for a female

Weight: 80.5 pounds for a male, 70.5 pounds for a female

Color: a light to red wheat color, darker muzzle and ears are permitted

The ridge is a strip of hair along the backbone that grows in the opposite direction to the rest of the coat.

European explorers of Africa mentioned the Hottentot dogs with a "ridge." White settlers crossed the indigenous dogs with their own gundogs. Because this dog was originally used for hunting lions, it is still sometimes referred to as the "lion-dog" today. Hunters used several of these dogs to track down the scent of a lion and then perform clever mock assaults to distract the lion, enabling the hunter to get close enough to shoot. This work demanded fearless, daredevil dogs with a lightning-quick response, enormous agility, and team spirit. This adaptable dog has a good bond with his humans. He is sometimes trained to hunt and has a good reputation thanks to his fine nose and love of retrieving. He is very intelligent, eager to learn, powerful, spirited, and needs consistent training. Experience and knowledge of canine behavior are necessary. Under this assumption, the ridgeback is a reliable, fascinating, easy-care, dependent family breed and a loyal guard dog and protector. The energetic, quick-moving dog loves to hunt using his eyes and nose; however, after careful training, he will always come back. He is not a dog for people with an inactive lifestyle.

71

Hungarian Pointing Dog

Shoulder height: 23–25 inches for a male, 21–23.5 inches for a female

Weight: 45–66 pounds for a male, 40–55 pounds for a female

Color: dark sandy gold to copper

The first water-trained scent hound in Germany was a Hungarian pointing dog.

Scent hounds arrived with the migration to the Carpathian Basin, known today as Hungary. This breed was later influenced by a yellow Turkish hunting dog. In the eighteenth century, this dog was selectively bred for the new hunting methods. Pointers and German short-haired pointers were crossed.

The Hungarian wirehaired pointer was a result of a crossing with the German wirehaired pointer; he is a robust gundog. The Hungarian short-haired pointer, also known as the Vizsla, is bred as a show dog. The Vizsla is willing to please and be docile; however, he can be quite an attention seeker. He is counted as one of the all-arounders of the gundogs that searches, points, retrieves, is an excellent tracking dog, and loves the water. He works very well in hot, dry weather. His versatility, great intelligence, and devotion make him an ideal companion for the recreational hunter, as long as he is brought up in an obedient yet loving household. The Vizsla is suitable for dog sports as well as outdoor pursuits such as disaster rescue training. This spirited, joyful dog needs to be given meaningful tasks and loves close contact with his people.

Bloodhounds

Bavarian Mountain Hound

Shoulder height: 18.5–20.5 inches for a male, 17–19 inches for a female

Weight: about 39.5–62 pounds

Color: deer red to reddish yellow, tan, reddish gray, brindled

Hanoverian Hound

Shoulder height: 19.5–22.5 inches for a male, 19–21 inches for a female

Weight: 66–88 pounds for a male, 55–77 pounds for a female

Color: light to dark deer red, brindled, with or without mask

These breeds scent track the blood of injured wildlife.

Bavarian Mountain Hound

An indispensable hunting assistant on difficult mountain terrain, the bloodhound scent tracks the blood of wounded animals and then alerts his owner to their presence by barking loudly. He was bred from a crossing between a Hanoverian hound in the late nineteenth century (this breed was too heavy for mountain work) and a Tyrolean hound. He was bred exclusively for searching for deer tracks, chamois, wild boar, and other game. This specialized gundog is very versatile, tough, and an excellent climber. He is very loyal, obedient, and sensitive.

Hanoverian Hound

This breed goes back to the ancient Celtic bracken dog that was bred in 500 B.C. to hunt deer. He emerged later from the strongest dogs of this breed that tracked down larger deer and boar, closely followed by riders with hounds that hunted and killed the animal. When hunting with guns began, he became specialized in searching for wounded or shot game. He also hunts fresh tracks before any shooting takes place. Breeding of the Hanoverian hound is subject to strict selection because of the high demands made on his service abilities. He is bred on request and only belongs to hunters.

Top: a Bavarian mountain hound

Left: a Hanoverian hound

73

Hounds

German Hound
Shoulder height: 16–21 inches

Weight: about 44 pounds

Color: red to yellow with black saddle and white muzzle, neck ring, chest, legs, and tip of tail

Slovakian Hound
Shoulder height: 18–19.5 inches for a male, 16–18 inches for a female

Weight: 33–44 pounds

Color: black and tan

Austrian Black and Tan Hound
Shoulder height: 19.5–22 inches for a male, 19–21 inches for a female

Weight: 33–49 pounds

Color: black with brownish red markings; a brown marking above each eye must be present

All hounds are robust and passionate. Some belong exclusively to hunters.

German Hound
Originating from several different hound breeds, this dog has been bred officially since 1900. The sensitive and mentally strong, quiet domestic dog is a passionate scent hound with great perseverance in field work and retrieving game. He is known as a forest working dog.

Slovakian Hound
The Slovakian hound is particularly good at hunting pigs. He possesses a remarkable sense of direction and is a good guard dog. He is a passionate, versatile, affectionate, and pleasant gundog.

Austrian Black and Tan Hound
The Austrian black and tan hound is an excellent bloodhound on the mountains. He is docile, a good flushing dog on land and water, and can learn to retrieve well.

From top to bottom: a German hound, a Slovakian hound, an Austrian black and tan hound

Coarse-Haired Styrian Hound

Shoulder height: 18.5–21 inches for a male, 18–20 inches for a female

Weight: 33–40 pounds

Color: red and pale yellow

Tyrolean Hound

Shoulder height: 17–19.6 inches for a male, 16.5-19 inches for a female

Weight: 33–48 pounds

Color: red or dark red, tricolor

Westphalian Dachsbracke

Shoulder height: 12–15 inches

Weight: 33 pounds

Color: same as German hound

Alpine Dachsbracke

Shoulder height: 13–16.5 inches

Weight: 33–40 pounds

Color: deer, dark deer red, black with rust or fire red

From top to bottom: an Alpine Dachsbracke, a Tyrolean hound, a Westphalian Dachsbracke

Right: a coarse-haired Styrian hound

Tyrolean Hound

This is an ideal working dog for hunting in the forest and mountains. This breed is used as a lone hound to hunt hare, fox, and other wild species.

Coarse-Haired Styrian Hound

This is the result of crossing the Hanoverian hound, the coarse-haired Istrian hound, and the Austrian black and tan hound. He is ideal for scent tracking on difficult terrain.

Westphalian Dachsbracke

This breed is mainly used for flushing out hare, fox, rabbit, and wild boar and also used for scent-tracking work.

Alpine Dachsbracke

This is an excellent bloodhound for hoofed game. He is too loud to hunt hare and fox. He is a persistent, calm dog with a fine nose, very good at tracking, and barks loudly when prey is found.

Different states have different laws on using hounds when hunting game.

Gundogs Without Handlers

Left: The Irish wolfhound and deerhound require plenty of space.

Right: The whippet is very affectionate and personable.

Far right: Playing games with dummy prey helps the beagle bond with his owner.

Bottom: Two Basset Griffon Vendéen (Grand and Petit)—these distinctive hounds have a mind of their own.

Wolves know all the tricks for hunting. Each individual animal in the pack has a particular skill, so the tasks are divided up, which ensures the survival of the pack. This skilled hunting behavior is deeply rooted in the genetic makeup of the dog, selectively bred by humans over many millennia; this has resulted in some breeds being hunting specialists. Gundogs were selectively bred according to hunting methods and available weapons used for the hunt. The history of gundogs is closely linked with the cultural history of humankind. In recent times, some dogs have proven themselves as family dogs, but they are still not the easiest dogs to own. A person has to understand the dog's behavior in order to decide whether this particular breed is right for his or her lifestyle. The beauty of these dogs can be a persuasive factor when purchasing a dog, but their innate behavior can cause a new owner a lot of stress.

Gundogs Without Handlers
Scent Hounds

Their task is to find a scent, track it, and flush out the game. They also pick up the prey and communicate by barking when prey is found. Because the nature of this work requires a dog whose skills are vastly superior to that of a human, people are not needed in this hunt. The hunter follows his dog and relies on the success of the dog.

Territorial boundaries are irrelevant. Dogs hunt together, but not in a well-organized pack. For the human-dog community, this means that the dogs work independently, have no inclination to be subordinate, and are not sensitive to the pecking order. Their territory is wherever it is possible to hunt. Therefore, they will not aggressively defend their social standing or their territorial boundaries. These avid hunters run off on the lookout for prey, which includes anything edible, and they are driven primarily by greed.

Sight Hounds (Greyhounds)

Greyhounds are sprinters that chase down their prey, catch it, and sometimes kill it. They have extremely good eyesight and do not miss even the slightest movement on the horizon. The Eastern European, Middle Eastern, and African greyhounds are independent long-range hunters. They played an important role

in the survival of human beings and were highly prized, but subordination and obedience were not required of them. They tended to be very unsophisticated in their pack behavior. They were only subordinate to their owner if she had proved herself to be a good pack leader; however, aggressive dogs were never tolerated. The dogs shared living quarters with their people and were more vigilant and restrained around strangers than scent-tracking dogs. Western greyhounds are short-distance sprinters used for hare and rabbit hunting. Close cohabitation with humans meant they were more willing to be subordinate and more personal than the other breeds. Western greyhounds are not constantly on the lookout for prey, but they do respond to wildlife that appears directly in front of them. Therefore, it is fine to let one of these dogs off the leash, provided he is well trained, because

he will not tend to go off and hunt on his own. This becomes more difficult with several dogs, which immediately create their own pack to hunt in. This also applies to those that were bred for racing. Greyhounds are calm in the home and more temperamental and spirited when outside. Mediterranean greyhounds display very primitive canine

behavior—always on the hunt and great lovers of freedom. The Spanish greyhound was bred from crossings between various greyhound breeds and is bred for commercial greyhound racing.

Beagle

Shoulder height: 13–16 inches

Weight: 20–25 pounds

Color: all hound colors except liver brown

Beagles are very robust; the dense fur is weatherproof and easy to maintain.

The Romans discovered the beagle in Britain. The breed was first given its name in 1475. In the sixteenth century, beagles accompanied English kings during the hunt. The beagle is considered the smaller version of the former Southern hound, derived from the French Bleu de Gascogne rabbit gundog. Because she is smaller and slower than the main pack of hounds, hunters go on foot rather than on horseback to hunt for hares. Today the beagle is kept as a pet, thanks to his pleasant characteristics. Adaptable, sociable, and friendly within a group, beagles are unfortunately deemed ideal for use in laboratories for animal testing. This small, colorful hound is gentle, cheerful, funny, and smart but also a bit stubborn. The beagle is never severe or aggressive. This passionate hound follows any and every scent trail only too happily; she is very strong willed and independent. Therefore, the beagle needs consistent training right from the start, which is difficult to enforce when she is a cute puppy, and often seems to be a waste of time when she discovers her first scent track. The biggest problem with this breed is that once she has found a scent, she forgets her obedience training in an instant and will follow her nose, much to the despair of her owner.

Basset Hound

Shoulder height: 13–15 inches

Weight: 44–64 pounds

Color: all hound colors permitted

The short-legged gene is a relatively common mutation in domestic dogs.

The basset hound is a descendant of the very sturdy, now extinct French Basset d'Artois and the lighter Basset Artesien Normand. Both were crossed in 1874 in England and merged into a single breed. In 1892, this breed was crossed with a bloodhound. The result was a basset hound, which was used for hunting rabbits in small packs, and proved to be particularly efficient in remote, dense forest areas. She has outstanding scent-tracking abilities. Years ago in the United States, these dogs fell into the hands of show breeders who exaggerated the features of the breed and created a caricature of the former hunting dog. She also came into vogue as the mascot for Hush Puppies brand shoes. Fortunately the trend did not last long because she is not the easiest of dogs to own. She hunts independently and is very stubborn. Owners need to be consistently patient when training this breed, and she is never very willing to obey commands. The calm, laid-back Basset is not fond of running and does not make a good guard dog.

Basset Griffon Vendéen

Shoulder height: *Petit:* 13–15 inches; *Grand:* 16–17 inches for a male, 15–17 inches for a female

Weight: *Petit:* 25–40 pounds; *Grand:* 40–44 pounds

Color: black with white spotting (white and black); black with tan markings (black and tan); fawn with white spotting (white and orange); fawn with black mantle and white spotting (tricolor); fawn or sand with black cloud-shaped markings; sand with black cloud-shaped markings and white spotting

"A devil in the countryside, an angel in the house" describes the petite breed. Both breeds are equally willful.

The French bassets are short-legged hounds whose breed dates back to the sixteenth century. The name comes from the French *bas*, meaning "deep or low." The short-legged gene is congenital; the dog has shorter leg bones due to a genetic mutation. Pictures of these short-legged dog breeds were found on monuments in ancient Egypt. They are identical to their normal-legged relatives in every way other than their short legs. Their funny, rough-around-the-edges appearance has won them many fans. There are two breeds of the Basset Griffon Vendéen: the Petit (small) and Grand (large). They are gentle when among the family, always in a good mood, lively, with seemingly inexhaustible endurance, speed, and power. This independent hunting dog is still an avid hunter and therefore unsuitable for people who just want a dog they can take on relaxing walks. The Grand primarily hunts hares; the Petit hunts rabbits. They differ not only in size, but also slightly in appearance. The fur must be groomed regularly; this breed sheds profusely.

Top: a Grand Basset Griffon Vendéen

Left: a Petit Basset Griffon Vendéen

Dalmatian

Shoulder height: 22–24 inches for a male, 21–23 inches for a female

Weight: 59.5–70.5 pounds for a male, 53–64 pounds for a female

Color: white with round, clearly defined, and evenly distributed black or brown spots

This dog can run at considerable speed without tiring.

Little is known about this breed's origins. It is classified in this group because of the similarities of its appearance and behavior. The spotted dog was known to the ancient Egyptians. She later became called a hound, but where she came from and what she hunted is unknown. Dalmatians were coach dogs and very popular in Victorian times. She lived in the stables and accompanied the carriages, where she usually ran under the rear axle. When the motorcar replaced the horse-drawn carriage, this decorative dog became a family dog. The Dalmatian is lively, spirited, happy, and quick and eager to learn. She is not aggressive but is vigilant and ready to defend in an emergency. She needs plenty of exercise and is a great dog for sporty people. However, her hound heritage should not be denied, and she must always be carefully supervised.

She came into fashion again after the release of the 1961 Walt Disney film *101 Dalmatians*. She is not the easiest dog to keep; she is not in any way suitable for people with an inactive lifestyle. Otherwise, she is uncomplicated and easy to care for. Puppies are born white; after a few days, the spots begin to appear.

81

Irish Wolfhound

Shoulder height: minimum 31 inches for a male, minimum 28 inches for a female

Weight: 120 pounds for a male, 89 pounds for a female

Color: gray, brindle, red, black, white, fawn, and all other deerhound colors

Their large size puts a strain on the organs causing this breed to have a short life expectancy of six to eight years.

The Romans wrote accounts of huge dogs in Ireland that were used for wolf and elk hunting. They were not only hunting companions but also constant, revered companions of chiefs and kings. Despite the export ban on popular dogs in the sixteenth century, the Irish wolfhound was virtually extinct by the nineteenth century. In 1860, English Captain George Augustus Graham recreated the powerful dog we know today with help from wolfhound bloodlines, deerhounds, German Great Danes, Borzois, and other large breeds. The unusual appearance of this breed soon made it very fashionable. Irish wolfhounds were marketed extensively, but the Irish giant is a demanding breed to rear and train due to her large size. Young animals must be carefully reared to avoid bone damage. Careful, selective breeding is essential to ensure a healthy dog. Nevertheless, their life expectancy is low. The sensitive giant is gentle, kind, and definitely not a guard dog. She is calm and peaceful in the house but loves to go on long walks. Her need for play is not particularly pronounced. She is not suitable for racing and very rarely courses, or pursues game by sight.

Deerhound

Shoulder height: minimum 30 inches for a male, minimum 28 inches for a female

Weight: 100 pounds for a male, 80.5 pounds for a female

Color: dark blue gray, darker and lighter gray or brindle and yellow; sandy red or reddish brown with a black mask and black ears, legs, and tail; a little white on the chest, toes, and tip of tail is permitted.

The coarse fur is easy to maintain and only sheds a little.

The Scottish deerhound is an aristocratic, noble breed and probably the purest descendant of the ancient Celtic greyhounds. Scottish clans bred the deerhound with the utmost care, for hunting wolves and large wildlife in the highlands. In 1746, the British beat the Scots in the Battle of Culloden and the clans disbanded, which threatened the survival of the deerhound. The breed owes its survival to Sir Walter Scott, an eighteenth-century poet, who placed all things Scottish on a pedestal in his poems and made the deerhound popular once again. In the nineteenth century, the famous artist Sir Edwin Landseer painted pictures of deerhounds. Then, when Queen Victoria became the proud owner of a deerhound, the breed was saved once and for all. The deerhound is gentle, never intrusive, quiet in the house, and obedient. When outdoors, this rugged runner shows her true temperament. The breed is expensive to keep and very time consuming. This large dog has a high life expectancy as long as she has plenty of space. She enjoys having a close bond with her family. She is a good courser but not suitable for the race track.

Greyhound

Shoulder height: 28–30 inches for a male, 27–28 inches for a female

Weight: 60–88 pounds for a male, 60–75 pounds for a female

Color: black, white, red, blue, brownish reddish yellow, buff, or brindle, any of these colors with white

Like with horse races, some people like to bet on greyhound races.

Greyhounds are considered to be the fastest dogs in the world. The short-distance runner can reach a speed of up to 37 miles per hour during a sprint! In 375 B.C., the Celts brought greyhounds with them to Britain. Greyhounds always enjoyed the special affection of their noblemen, and there are many accounts of this breed dating back hundreds of years. The greyhound was used in England for the coursing, in which two greyhounds chased a live hare. They were later used for track racing behind an artificial hare. People bet large sums of money on the dogs. The greyhound became an object of profit that was doomed once her racing career was over. Animal shelters rehome many of these unfortunate animals.

Greyhounds are loving, cuddly, quiet in the household, unassuming, and easy to care for. They are in great need of a close family bond and a loving upbringing to make them obedient companions. Their innate prey drive makes letting them off the leash in a wildlife-rich area problematic. Greyhounds love racing and coursing, but they are also bred as show dogs.

Whippet

Shoulder height: 18.5–20 inches for a male, 17–18.5 inches for a female

Weight: 15–30 pounds

Color: all

The whippet is a clean, easy-to-care-for dog.

The whippet was bred by miners and factory workers in the north of England and contributed to family life by catching rabbits. Besides poaching, she earned betting money for rabbit catching in closed arenas, and when that was made illegal, she took part in track racing. In the old days, this involved the owner waving a towel at his dog at the end of the track. The whippet is a quiet, sensitive housemate; tenderly devoted to her family; lively; cheerful; playful outdoors; and always ready to join in with whatever her owner is doing. This intelligent dog should be trained lovingly. However, one should not underestimate her personality. The whippet is very affectionate and loves close physical contact with her people but is never intrusive and is more reserved toward strangers. She gets her territorial instinct from the terrier, and she is ever vigilant. This short-distance sprinter loves to play by herself or with other whippets, and she enjoys a game of Frisbee® or agility classes. Because she is obedient and stays by her owner's side, you can let her off the leash, as long as she does not have a racing background, and as long as there is no wildlife directly under her nose. Coursing is preferable to track racing for health reasons.

Afghan Hound

Shoulder height: 27–29 inches for a male, 25–27 inches for a female

Weight: 60 pounds for a male, 50 pounds for a female

Color: all colors permitted

Coursing is an activity very similar to real-life hunting.

The Afghan is considered one of the most beautiful breeds. Afghans tend to hunt on their own or in pairs and chase whatever is on the land, from hares to gazelles to leopards. The Afghan hound has preserved this independent hunting streak even today. These dogs came to England with British officers at the end of the nineteenth century. Initially, the desert type (called the Bell-Murray strain) and the mountainous Afghan (Ghazni strain) were favored for breeding. But the desert racer was considered less attractive because it had less fur, so the Ghazni became the most popular breed. This proud, intelligent dog does not ask for affection and needs a sensitive owner because normal training methods have little success. The owner must be a prudent leader but will find it difficult to prove himself as he will never be able to hunt as well as the dog! The Afghan hound needs a lot of exercise but cannot be let off the leash because of her innate prey drive. A large area of land secured by a fence is the best option, and keeping several dogs is a good idea. Coursing is an ideal hunting substitute. The beautiful, silky fur needs a lot of care.

Saluki

Shoulder height: 23–28 inches for a male, smaller for a female

Weight: 35–65 pounds

Color: all colors and color combinations, except brindle; the short-haired variety without feathering is very rare

Other than having to groom the long fur on the ears and tail, this breed is easy to care for.

According to the Muslim holy book, the Koran, "The Saluki is not a dog, he is a gift from Allah, for our benefit and our joy." Also known as the Persian greyhound, this dog has been around for many millennia throughout the East, from China to Arabia, Egypt, and Turkey. Depending on the region, he has coarse or smooth hair, varying in length on the ears, legs, right down to his feathered tail. The Saluki—most likely named after the old Arab city of Saluq—is a long-distance runner. He rode on horseback and sat in front of the hunter. As soon as he spotted wild falcon, the Saluki would calmly leap from the horse and hunt the falcon to a standstill. He hunted everything: rabbits, gazelles, ostriches, onagers (Asiatic wild ass), wolves, foxes, and jackals. He arrived in England with Arabian horses in 1700. This low-key, sensitive dog likes to stay very close to his owner during the hunt. His need to hunt can be satisfied by coursing or racing. He is quiet in the home and a playful, lively dog outdoors. With plenty of love and praise, he can learn to be an obedient well-trained member of the household. However, when he spots prey, he will forget everything he has ever been taught. The Saluki is reserved with strangers, but he is not shy nor aggressive. This dignified dog is intelligent and independent.

Sloughi and Azawakh

Sloughi

Shoulder height: 26–28 inches for a male, 24–27 inches for a female

Weight: 55–65 pounds for a male, 35–50 pounds for a female

Color: light sand to fawn, with or without black mask, with or without black mantle, with or without black brindle, with or without black overlay

Azawakh

Shoulder height: 25–29 inches for a male, 23.5–27.5 inches for a female

Weight: 44–55 pounds for a male, 33–44 pounds for a female

Color: light sand to dark fawn, also brindled, with or without black mask and/or blaze, white spot on chest, tip of tail, and paws

Both breeds can still be found in their original habitats.

Top: a Sloughi

Right: an Azawakh

Sloughi

Also known as the Arabian greyhound, this dog is seen as precious a possession as any horse or camel to the Bedouin people. These dogs live as revered family members in the tents. They are suspicious of strangers and always ready to defend. During the hunt, the dog leaps from a galloping horse once she has spotted the fleeing game, then hunts down the game. Today this form of hunting is prohibited. The Sloughi requires a very sensitive upbringing, and is a quiet and clean housemate, provided she has access to a large fenced property, can play with her peers, and regularly participates in coursing or racing.

Azawakh

As fast as the wind, as persistent as the camel, and as beautiful as the Arabian horse—so is the graceful greyhound of the Tuareg, the nomads of the south Sahara. The dog's duties are to hunt and to guard. Originally a wild breed, she is reserved with strangers and affectionate to those she loves. The proud, independent hunting dog needs to be trained with plenty of love and patience. A good knowledge of canine behavior is required. Being overly strict makes her uncertain, and if you fail as a pack leader, she will never forgive you.

Borzoi

Shoulder height: 29.5–33.5 inches for a male, 27–31 inches for a female

Weight: 75–105 pounds for a male, 60–90 pounds for a female

Color: all colors except blue and chocolate brown; solid or colored blotches

The silky, soft wavy to curly fur needs regular grooming.

The ancestors of these Russian greyhounds were brought from the East by the Tatars. Since the start of Tsarist rule in the fourteenth century, the Borzoi was bred to hunt hares, foxes, and wolves. During the October Revolution in 1917, the people destroyed almost all dogs of the hated nobility. The Borzoi in Russia was threatened with extinction, but now she is owned by many wealthy European and American citizens worldwide. Her essence is characterized by noble composure and restraint. She is a very pleasant, gentle family dog that needs close contact with her people and her home. She can be easily trained as long as the training is carried out with love and care; she does not respond to severity. This quiet dog rarely barks in the house yet has an innate protective instinct. She is unapproachable for strangers. She shows little interest in other dogs; however, if she is provoked, she is an uncompromising opponent with tremendous strength and agility. This athletic dog needs a lot of running, which can be problematic due to her passion for hunting. She also loves coursing and track racing.

Italian Greyhound

Shoulder height: 12.5–15 inches

Weight: maximum 11 pounds

Color: solid black, slate gray, beige, white on chest and feet permitted

The fur is too thin to keep out the cold and dampness. This breed should live purely as an indoor dog.

The Italian greyhound is the smallest of the greyhound breeds and can be traced back to ancient times. She was the favorite of kings and noble ladies. The most famous Italian greyhound fan was undoubtedly Frederick the Great, King of Prussia, who loved his dog more than anything. The small greyhound, which looks so delicate with her paws tucked in, always seems to look as if she is freezing cold. Despite her appearance, she is a hardy, dedicated hunter and racer due to her natural breeding. She needs a lot of exercise. She should make an obedient companion with loving and consistent training. She does not like to stray too far from her owner, so she can be let off the leash. This breed can be kept well in a group, even in limited space, because she loves to have close contact with her people. Her unexpectedly strong personality and courage belie her small size. The greyhound is a fun, lively housemate; however, she is not a good pet for small children. She has a remarkably high life expectancy of twelve to fifteen years.

Mediterranean Greyhounds

Spanish Greyhound

Shoulder height: 24.5–27.5 inches for a male, 23.5–27 inches for a female

Weight: 60 pounds for a male, 50–55 pounds for a female

Color: all; coarse-haired or short-haired coats

Podenco

Shoulder height: varies according to type, for example, Ibizan hound: 26–28 inches for a male, 24–26 inches for a female

Weight: 42–55 pounds

Color: red and white, solid white or red, yellow; coarse-haired or smooth-haired coats

These breeds are often rescued by animal welfare organizations.

Spanish Greyhound

This dog can still be found hunting rabbits and guarding farms in Andalusia and Castile. Greyhound breeds were crossed with Spanish greyhounds for professional racing. The purebred Spanish greyhound is a fast, persistent hunter. As a companion, she is quiet and affectionate, yet aggressive toward strangers. She is very vigilant and attentive at all times. Retired racing dogs are often saved from a cruel fate by animal welfare organizations, where they are cared for and then rehomed in loving households.

Podenco

Throughout the Mediterranean, from the Canary Islands to Crete, you will find this breed, which has been around since ancient times. Podencos are still used for hunting and have very good retrieving skills. They are well adapted to rough terrain and climate of their homeland. This independent hunter, which does not tend to have a close bond with humans, is a difficult dog to own. She needs an owner with a lot of patience and very good knowledge of canine behavior. However, she will always remain independent and is driven by her innate hunting passion. Many Podencos are rescued and rehomed.

Top: a Spanish greyhound

Left: an Ibizan hound (Podenco)

91

Independent Hunters

Left: A Jack Russell terrier hunts between glacial boulders.

Right: The dachshund has become a favorite family pet.

Far right: The German hunting terrier is a very passionate, aggressive, independent hunter and is not suitable as a family dog.

This particular group includes many fascinating companion dogs. These independent breeds all have one thing in common: they are bred to hunt and catch their prey and then kill it. As "do-it-yourself" dogs, they have a weak social pack instinct. They are used specifically to hunt certain prey; they are sent down narrow rabbit burrows, for example. They will vehemently defend their hunting territory and hunt wild animals such as foxes, badgers, martens, otters, and rats—all very powerful animals that put up a strong fight. The word *terrier* means "under the earth."

Terriers were originally bred in England. Each part of the country had its own breed for a specific purpose. Foxes hunt newborn lambs to feed their newborn litters and so were hunted by terriers. Terriers also hunt in the barren mountain regions with thin topsoil in between glacial boulders. The little terrier scurries into the narrow gaps with no hope of help from her owner. If she comes across a fox, she will fight it to the death, or be killed herself. Only the toughest, cleverest dogs survive. Badgers and otters were formerly popular game animals, and rat catching brought good money. Terriers were valuable members of the household; the more swashbuckling the better. They were not asked to be subordinate and were totally dominant when performing their duties. During foxhunting, a leisure activity of wealthy Britons, the terrier is trained to drive the fox uninjured out of hiding so she does not spoil the fun of the hunt. The German equivalent of English terriers are the dachshunds. As a short-legged hound, she is not only a dashing

fighter under the earth (due to being crossbred with the terrier), but she is also very useful for other hunting duties, such as foraging and searching for wounded wildlife.

Some terriers, as well as the schnauzer and pinscher, lived in stables. Before the automobile, the horse was the

most important form of transportation. These were fantastic times for rats and mice because they would eat the horse feed. The dogs caught the rodents quickly and efficiently and defended their territories vigorously against intruders—horses were coveted possessions. This type of dog was required to hunt with no cooperation from the owner or other dogs. The skill of the individual accounted for the success; besides, rats and mice could hardly be shared among a pack. The dogs did not have a strong bond with their people. Their hunting skills were innate, so training them to hunt was not necessary. People came in and out of the stables and often had little interaction with the dog. Humans did not really need to earn the trust of a rat catcher. For dog owners today, this means headstrong dogs that assert themselves,

are not afraid to use their teeth, and will do so successfully. They do not like strange dogs and are very argumentative within a pack; this can be seen from very early on in the litter of puppies.

Terriers are distrustful of strangers; however, as clever opportunists, they learn to allow themselves to be stroked if it

means they get treats. They are vigilant and not afraid to bite if they feel the need. Terriers can give the experienced owner plenty of joy and are ideal for the confident person who is not easily upset. These clever dogs quickly understand how far they can go and can be easily trained to obey, but only to the one that they recognize as a boss. If given a chance to assert themselves, they will quickly become the lovable rogue who does what she likes. These dogs also have no problem with people who pet them and allow them to dominate the household, which is more common than you may think. Many people allow these dogs to take charge without actually realizing what is happening to the human-dog relationship. This is not as much of a serious problem for a small breed as it would be for a large breed.

Dachshund

Weight: *standard type:* about 20 pounds

Chest circumference: *standard:* 14 inches; *miniature:* 12–14 inches; *rabbit dachshund:* up to 12 inches

Color: *long-haired and smooth-haired coats:* solid red, reddish yellow, yellow with or without black hairs; two-tone black or brown with tan or yellow markings; dappled; *wirehaired coat:* predominantly wild boar color, otherwise same as long-haired and smooth-haired varieties

All dachshund breeds are easy to care for, but the long-haired breeds need regular grooming.

The dachshund originates from short-legged hound breeds. Her short legs allow her to forage in dense vegetation. She is relatively slow, so she can be easily tracked by the hunter and slip into badger and fox holes. This purebred bloodhound is amazingly versatile; she uses her powerful body to fight underground against the fox. She forages for game, is skilled at scenting blood, and can also be used for water work. Despite her passion for hunting, she is a popular companion dog. The clown, the prankster, the actor among dogs never gets bored, and her facial expressions are inimitable. She knows exactly how to wrap her human around her little paw. She is affectionate, considerate, brash, and a little daredevil whenever the situation demands.

Previous page, top: a wild-boar-colored wirehaired standard dachshund

Previous page, bottom left: a wild-boar-colored wirehaired miniature dachshund

Previous page, bottom right: a red long-haired rabbit dachshund

Left: a red long-haired standard dachshund

Below: a red and black smooth-haired standard dachshund and a dappled smooth-haired standard dachshund

This watchful breed is always ready on the defense and knows how to earn her owner's respect. Because the dog's duties depend on her being able to work independently, one should not mistake her innate stubborn will for disobedience. Consistent, loving training will make her an obedient housemate. The main problem with this breed is that owners tend to become blinded by her charms and do not stick to their guns when training her. The wire-haired dachshund has plenty of terrier blood in her character. The distinctive, elegant smooth-haired type is very popular. The long-haired dachshund is a beautiful variety. Dachshunds have several different sizes, defined by chest circumference, and come in many colors.

Cairn Terrier and West Highland White Terrier

Cairn Terrier

Shoulder height: 11–12 inches

Weight: 13–16.5 pounds

Color: red, cream, wheaten, gray or almost black, brindle

West Highland White Terrier

Shoulder height: about 11 inches

Weight: about 15 pounds

Color: white

The coarse fur of the cairn is easy to care for and can be trimmed into shape.

These dogs were bred to hunt, not for sport but out of necessity; they hunted foxes that killed lambs belonging to shepherds. In the thin topsoil of the Scottish Highlands, the fox lives in between glacial boulders in cairns, man-made piles of stone. Only the toughest terriers survived their duty to kill the fox. White puppies were culled because they were seen to be inferior. However, Major Edward Donald Malcolm from Poltalloch took to breeding them. His dogs were shown to be just as good as the colored cairns and were officially recognized as the **West Highland white terrier**, or Westie, in 1904. Both breeds are confident and always happy, but as typical terriers, do not get along with members of the same sex. They are self-sufficient but not stubborn. They are quick to learn but do need consistent training; otherwise, they will try to dominate the pack. They are alert but do not bark unnecessarily. They make good city dogs if kept in pairs or groups because they will keep one another entertained. The Westie will only remain a beautiful white color with plenty of grooming. Her fur should be kept trimmed.

Top: a Westie

Right: a cairn terrier

Scottish Terrier and Skye Terrier

Scottish Terrier

Shoulder height: 10–11 inches

Weight: 19–23 pounds

Color: black, wheaten, brindle in any color

Skye Terrier

Shoulder height: 10 inches, length from nose to tip of tail: 40.5 inches

Weight: 35–40 pounds for a male, 25–30 pounds for a female

Color: gray, fawn, cream with black marks on ears and muzzle, black

Both breeds are alert but not loud and have a strong urge to run.

Scottish Terrier

Various different Scottish terrier breeds were developed in secluded valleys and on Scottish islands. Captain Gordon Murray bred a sociable dog from the traditional hunting dog that was no longer required to perform her original duties. She became a fashionable breed in the United States. The Scottie is a quiet, serious dog that finds it difficult to befriend strangers. She is loyal to her family, but she still has a strong personality. The coat should be trimmed.

Skye Terrier

The terrier from the Isle of Skye in northwest Scotland is an unusual phenomenon. This fierce hunter has been paraded in the show ring for many centuries. She no longer hunts foxes but still has to be discouraged from doing so when on walks. She has a difficult personality and is maintenance intensive. She will only obey the one she has accepted as her master or mistress. She is suspicious of strangers. She is an enormously powerful dog, despite her short legs, and is very protective. If you are a fan of dogs with a self-reliant, lone-wolf nature, then this is the dog for you.

Top: a Scottish terrier

Right: a Skye terrier

Norfolk Terrier and Norwich Terrier

Shoulder height: 10 inches

Weight: 10–12 pounds

Color: red, wheaten, gray or black and tan or grizzle

The natural look is more desirable; these breeds should not look coiffed or "overdone."

The **Norwich terrier** has erect ears; the **Norfolk terrier's** ears flop forward. In the 1960s, these two breeds were crossed. They come from the southern English county of Norfolk, whose capital is Norwich, which is a fertile agricultural region. Farmers used these little terriers to catch rats, mice, and rabbits. They were also used to hunt badgers and foxes. It is suspected they are related to the cairn and Scottish terriers. University students in Cambridge made them popular. To pass the time, the dogs accompanied the students on hunts for muskrats and house rats in the numerous channels around the city. The dogs had to share small accommodations with students; these little dogs proved themselves to be adaptable and unobtrusive. They are confident, lively, robust, and always cheerful. As excellent family dogs, their tender, amiable, and docile natures leave little to be desired. This dog makes a good city dog as long as you can keep her with you all day and provide her with plenty of exercise. The coarse fur has to be kept trim so that it does not shed and is easy to care for.

Top: a Norwich terrier

Right: a Norfolk terrier

Australian Terrier

Shoulder height: about 10 inches for a male; the female is shorter

Weight: 14 pounds for a male; the female weighs less

Color: blue and tan, sandy, or red

Despite her short legs, the Australian terrier is a sporty dog that loves to exercise.

The first settlers of Australia not only brought their belongings over with them on ships, but they also brought rats, which spread like wildfire on the newly discovered continent. Small terriers were led onto the ships for rat and mouse control. Scotland and Irish immigrants also kept their indispensable little helpers onboard. The short-legged, coarse-haired dogs with their steel-gray coats were famous for their incorruptible vigilance. In Australia, they were bred with all possible terriers, including the Irish Glen of Imaal terrier and Skye terrier—which may have contributed to the blue color—and the Norwich terrier. The Australian terriers were bred for work on the farms and in the settlements to keep down the rat population. Breeding for aesthetic reasons did not begin until the late nineteenth century. The Australian terrier is a robust,

adventurous, happy dog that is also intelligent and affectionate. She is sociable in a group. She is alert with strangers but not aggressive. She is easy to train and will give an inexperienced owner a lot of joy. The coat should be kept trimmed. The fur on the paws should be kept short.

Cesky Terrier and Sealyham Terrier

Cesky Terrier

Shoulder height: 10–12.5 inches (ideal 11.5 inches) for a male, 10.5 inches for a female

Weight: 13–22 pounds

Color: gray blue and light coffee, with lighter markings

Sealyham Terrier

Shoulder height: maximum 12 inches

Weight: 20 pounds for a male, 18 pounds for a female

Color: solid white; white with yellow, brown, blue, or badger-colored (brown and black) flecks on the head and ears

The silky fur of the Cesky can be cut into shape, which makes it easier to care for.

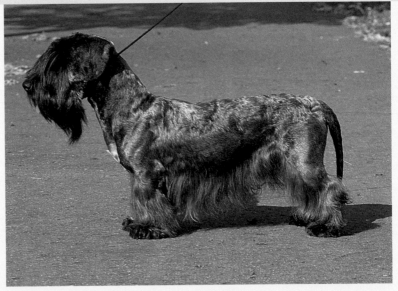

Cesky Terrier

The Czechoslovakian scientist Frantisek Horak was looking for a passionate, but not too aggressive, independent terrier. In 1949, he crossed the docile Sealyham with the aggressive Scottish terrier and created a lightweight, fast-moving, easygoing and docile terrier with an innate passion for hunting. In 1963, the breed was officially recognized. Today the Cesky is a great apartment dog; she is clean, small, and alert but does not bite. Quiet and adaptable, affectionate and obedient, she is suitable for older people who cannot walk long distances. Her attachment to her people means her hunting passion presents few problems. Her fur needs a lot of grooming.

Sealyham Terrier

At the end of the nineteenth century, Captain John Edwardes in Sealyham, Wales, bred fearless hunters for badgers, otters, weasels, skunks, and rabbits. Sealyham terriers were bred to be sociable with other dogs. The modern Sealyham is solid, plump, and has dense fur; she loves to hunt, yet she is a pleasant, cheerful housemate that also likes to play and run. She is friendly, docile, fearless, and attentive. Her deep voice is like that of a large dog, which makes her a good guard dog. She is reserved toward strangers. Her fur needs to be kept trimmed.

Top: a Cesky terrier

Right: a Sealyham terrier

Bedlington Terrier and Dandie Dinmont Terrier

Bedlington Terrier
Shoulder height: about 16 inches
Weight: 17.5–23 pounds
Color: blue, liver, and sandy with or without tan

Dandie Dinmont Terrier
Shoulder height: 8–11 inches
Weight: 17.5–24 pounds
Color: mustard, pepper

Blue Bedlington puppies are born with black fur.

Bedlington Terrier

This terrier was bred by English mining families in Bedlington to hunt wild rabbits and otters for their valuable furs. The dog also earned money for his people as a rat catcher. The Dandie Dinmont terrier is a close relative of this breed, among others. Only show dogs are sheared. His sweet, outward appearance is somewhat misleading: he is a keen hunter and tough fighter. He is intelligent, eager to learn, very versatile, and easy to train. The watchful, edgy four-legged member of the household is a very pleasant companion dog. He does not shed, provided he is groomed regularly. The fur can be easily trimmed into shape.

Dandie Dinmont Terrier

This terrier breed was named after the fictional character Dandie Dinmont, who kept this terrier breed as a pet in Sir Walter Scott's 1815 novel *Guy Mannering*. The success of the book at the end of the nineteenth century led to this breed becoming a popular pet in England's finest circles. He was known as the philosopher among terriers, quiet when the situation called for yet otherwise very lively. The Dandie is aloof with strangers but is affectionate and sociable with his family. He is an alert dog with a bark that commands respect. He is still kept as a rat catcher today. This is an ideal breed for a thoughtful, quiet person. The coat should be regularly groomed and trimmed into shape but not coiffed.

Top: a Bedlington terrier

Left: a Dandie Dinmont terrier

Welsh Terrier and Lakeland Terrier

Welsh Terrier

Shoulder height: maximum 15 inches

Weight: 20–21 pounds

Color: black and tan, grizzle and tan

Lakeland Terrier

Shoulder height: maximum 14.5 inches

Weight: 17 pounds for a male, 15 pounds for a female

Color: black and tan, blue and tan, red, wheaten, red grizzle, liver brown, blue, or black

The tan color refers to the brown markings on the legs and head.

Welsh Terrier

In Wales, this breed participated in foxhunts. His job was to flush the fox uninjured from the burrow. The Welsh terrier is a valiant, swashbuckling typical terrier. He is cheerful and amiable to his family. This popular terrier is often described as the "small Airedale."

As long as these breeds are given sufficient exercise and meaningful tasks, both the Lakeland and the Welsh terriers can be kept in the city. The Welsh terrier is often incompatible with same-sex dogs and not ideal in a group. As typical terriers, they need consistent training. They are docile but not always willing to submit. Neither breed sheds if trimmed regularly.

Lakeland Terrier

This breed originates from the Lake District in England, an area with plenty of sheep that need protection from foxes. This terrier was bred to keep the fox population down. The terrier is set upon the fox burrows to kill the fox. They were bred as show dogs from 1912, but they were still bred for hunting as well.

Today the Lakeland is a good family dog. He is vigilant, small, easy to care for, always happy, and cheerful, but he will not go out of his way to avoid a fight!

Top: a Welsh terrier

Right: a Lakeland terrier

Airedale Terrier

Shoulder height: 23–24 inches for a male, 22–23 inches for a female

Weight: 50–65 pounds for a male, 40–45 pounds for a female

Color: tan with black or grizzle on the saddle, neck, and top side of tail

The puppies are born with black and yellow markings that gradually lighten.

The "King of Terriers" is from the Aire Valley in central England. He is thought to be the result of crossing an otter hound with another aggressive terrier breed. He loves water and hunts otters, water voles, pine martens, skunks, and waterfowl. Thanks to careful selection, the Airedale terrier developed into an extremely robust, versatile, and utilitarian dog. He became famous worldwide as a first aid and messenger dog in both world wars, earning him the title of "war dog." It seems there is nothing the Airedale cannot do: guide dog, rescue dog, avalanche dog, gundog, and family dog. He is spirited but not nervous, inquisitive, and easy to train. He is alert and will display his protective instinct when required. He needs meaningful tasks and consistent training. An owner must be able to see through the dog's charm and show strong leadership. Only a little knowledge of canine behavior is necessary. He is not a dog for people with an inactive lifestyle, nor is he suited to life in the city. One advantage is that he does not shed as long as his fur is trimmed regularly.

Irish Terrier and Irish Glen of Imaal Terrier

Irish Terrier

Shoulder height: 18 inches

Weight: 27 pounds for a male, 25 pounds for a female

Color: solid red

Irish Glen of Imaal Terrier

Shoulder height: maximum 14 inches

Weight: 35 pounds, females weigh less

Color: blue, brindle, or wheaten

The wiry coat should be trimmed regularly to prevent it from shedding.

Irish Terrier

Like all Irish terriers, the "Red Devil" was bred to his current appearance in remote areas. These terriers were once brazen badger hunters. His attitude seems to be "victory or death!" He has an excellent reputation as a ratter and rabbit hunter. He pursues the rabbit without hesitation through the thorny scrub and chases rats in the water. The irresistible charm of the Irish terrier is due to his bravado and devotion to his people. He could be described as a tenderhearted hothead!

This intelligent dog has a strong character and needs consistent training, preferably of the physical kind, such as dog sports training, agility, and gundog training. He will not avoid a fight but face it head-on. Irish terrier dogs are strenuous and not suitable for leisurely strolls because they do not submit willingly and tend to follow their own interests. They need an owner with a natural air of authority who is happy to spend plenty of time outdoors exercising with him. He is a tireless companion. He is always cheerful, always on the go—the ideal dog for people who hate being bored.

Irish Glen of Imaal Terrier

The tough, feisty, disheveled terrier from the Imaal valley hunts badgers, foxes, and otters. He needs consistent training and is courageous when required but otherwise gentle and docile.

Top: an Irish terrier

Left: an Irish Glen of Imaal terrier

Irish Soft-Coated Wheaten Terrier and Kerry Blue Terrier

Irish Soft-Coated Wheaten Terrier

Shoulder height: 18–19 inches for a male, the female is shorter

Weight: 39.5–45 pounds for a male, the female weighs less

Color: every shade from light wheat to red gold

Kerry Blue Terrier

Shoulder height: 18–19.5 inches for a male, 17.5–19 inches for a female

Weight: 33–39.5 pounds for a male, the female weighs less

Color: blue, with or without black mask and ears

Some Wheaten terriers do not develop their adult coats until 2.5 years of age.

Irish Soft-Coated Wheaten Terrier

This dog had to earn his food on the farm. The all-around hunter fed off rats and mice, herded cattle, guarded the house and farm, and helped in all aspects of hunting. He is a cheerful and spirited housemate, loves people, and is alert but not aggressive. Affectionate and clever, he can be easily trained with love and consistency. He needs to be kept busy with meaningful tasks and plenty of exercise. The coat is not maintenance intensive and is easier to care for when trimmed.

Kerry Blue Terrier

He hails from the "Ring of Kerry" region where he guarded lonely farms, kept down the rat and mice population, and herded cattle. The Kerry blue terrier is a dog that can do anything and everything.

He is docile and a reliable guard dog that only barks when necessary. He has a pronounced territorial instinct and is intolerant toward strange dogs. He does not shed, and his silky coat must be trimmed to keep its shape.

Top: an Irish soft-coated wheaten terrier

Left: a Kerry blue terrier

105

Border Terrier

Shoulder height: 13–16 inches for a male, 11–14 inches for a female

Weight: 13–15.5 pounds for a male, 11–14 pounds for a female

Color: red, wheaten, ash (grizzle) and tan, blue and tan

Regular trimming prevents the fur from shedding.

The border terrier originates from the border area of England and Scotland and participated in the Border Hunt, a hunt involving a pack of hounds racing at breakneck speed. The pack was accompanied by the border terrier whose job was to drive the fox out of his burrow into the daylight. The aesthetic appearance of this dog was unimportant. Only his build and fur were critical. He had to be able to keep up with the horses, and his chest had to be narrow enough to get inside fox burrows. His fur had to be waterproof and protective, and his teeth strong enough to kill otters and badgers. The border terrier still hunts in Great Britain, but he has become more of a show dog and family dog nowadays. He is friendly with other dogs and is a good choice for a second dog. The border terrier is sociable, smart, tough, and easy to care for. This rugged, outdoorsy dog with the balanced temperament can be easily trained. He is, however, an independent hunter and will go his own way if unsupervised. He is a good companion for athletic people because he loves variety and exercise.

Manchester Terrier

Shoulder height: 16 inches for a male, 15 inches for a female

Weight: 18 pounds for a male, 17 pounds for a female

Color: black and tan

This breed can be kept in the city as long as he is given sufficient exercise and meaningful tasks.

These smooth-haired, black and tan terriers have existed in Britain for centuries. This breed is regarded as the ancestors for many of today's terrier breeds and also most likely the German pinscher. They were used for animal fighting. In the mining regions, he was used for killing rats, which also became a popular and lucrative sport; the more rats a dog killed, the more valuable he was.

These famous rat killers were also good at killing rabbits and were crossbred with the whippet in Manchester, resulting in a more elegant, faster breed of terrier. It was in this area of England that dog shows first began, so he became a popular show dog in the early days. He is rather rare in Manchester nowadays, despite the fact that he is actually a very pleasant companion dog. Manchester terriers have always lived closely with humans; they were kept in small numbers in people's homes, rather than in kennels. This breed is very domesticated, friendly, and easy to care for. His fine coat does not protect him from cold temperatures, but as long as he keeps moving he does not feel the cold. He is vigilant but not snappy, spirited, and loves to exercise, but he does not need to be kept constantly busy. Docile and easy to train, he is a joy for inexperienced dog owners.

Jack Russell Terrier and Parson Russell Terrier

Jack Russell Terrier

Shoulder height: ideal 10–12 inches

Weight: 11–13 pounds

Coat: smooth-coated, rough-coated, broken-coated varieties

Color: white with black and/or tan markings

Parson Russell Terrier

Shoulder height: ideal 14 inches for a male, ideal 13 inches for a female

Weight: 14–18 pounds

Coat: smooth-coated, rough-coated, broken-coated varieties

Color: white with tan, lemon, or black markings on the head and/or base of tail

Both breeds have always been popular in Great Britain even before they were given official recognition.

This is an old breed that embodies the archetype of the fox terrier, before it became a styled show dog. Parson John (Jack) Russell, born in 1795, was a passionate hunter and dog breeder who bred fox terriers as show dogs as well as bright white, robust hunting terriers. They were not bred to a particular standard of beauty but enjoyed great popularity with hunters and horsemen, who used them to hunt rats and mice and also used them for foxhunting. Their appearance and character were very unique, and because they became fashionable, they were bred senselessly and profusely. This is why there are so many aggressive examples today. Both terrier types are exceptionally lively, dashing, very independent, and determined. Nevertheless, they should be sociable and not snappy. Jack Russell terriers are smart, vigilant, very robust, and always on the go—not a breed for inactive or nervous people. This dog makes an ideal companion for a person with a similarly strong personality. Dividing this breed into two separate breeds was a purely political decision.

Top: a Jack Russell terrier

Right: a Parson Russell terrier

Fox Terrier

Shoulder height: *wire-haired:* maximum 15.5 inches for a male, the female is shorter

Weight: *wire-haired:* 18 pounds for a male, the female is somewhat less; *smooth-haired:* 16–18 pounds for a male, 15–17 pounds for a female

Color: *wire-haired:* white with black, black and tan, or tan markings; *smooth-haired:* all white, white with tan, black and tan, or black markings

The smooth-haired and wire-haired fox terriers became separate breeds in the United States in 1984.

**Top: a wire-haired fox terrier
Below: a smooth-haired version**

Used for foxhunting in Britain, these terriers are not supposed to kill the fox, but drive him from his hiding place uninjured so that the hunt can continue. Bright white dogs are preferred because they are in sharp contrast to the fox. These terriers are confident and have a great passion for hunting. They are intelligent, enterprising, happy, very docile, and alert companions. The fox terrier is a tough, rugged dog that likes to be busy and will not fight with his peers. He is extremely dominant and must be given consistent training, or he will become the boss of the house. Despite this, he is very charming and those who have won his affection will find him to be a tender and clingy housemate when he wants attention. The smooth-haired fox terrier is more dashing and somewhat tougher than the wire-haired, which became very fashionable, and so has changed somewhat over the years due to selective breeding. The wire-haired fox terrier does not shed as long as he has been professionally groomed, which also keeps the color of his fur bright and pure white. The smooth-haired fox terrier is easy to care for, but his fur sheds.

109

Schnauzer and Pinscher

Schnauzer

Shoulder height: 18–19.5 inches

Weight: 31–44 pounds

Color: black, salt and pepper

Pinscher

Shoulder height: 18–19.5 inches

Weight: 31–44 pounds

Color: red and black with red markings

Regular trimming prevents the schnauzer's coat from shedding.

The former "rat pinscher" lived in stables and barns, where he hunted rats and mice and guarded the yard. The "old German farm dog" was mainly found in Southern Germany. In 1882, the dog breeder Max Hartstein from Württemberg began to breed these dogs selectively; he emphasized the lush beard, eyebrows, and pure gray color. The short-haired variant, which was often found in a litter of wire-haired puppies, remained in the shadow of his bearded brothers. Pinschers were bred in colors that were culled in the schnauzer breed. Wagoners appreciated the clean dog; when they had a pinscher on the cart, no one dared to touch the horse or the cart. After World War II, it took a huge amount of effort to save this breed from extinction. Both breeds are self-confident, undaunted, and also need a confident, consistent owner who can sympathize with their friendly determination. These reliable guard dogs are intolerant of strange dogs and are aloof with strangers. In the family, however, he is devoted and enterprising. He will not tolerate unnecessary hardship nor someone who is too soft. Schnauzers occasionally show their hunting instincts; the pinscher more frequently so.

Top: a salt-and-pepper schnauzer

Right: a red pinscher

Doberman

Shoulder height: 27–28 inches for a male, 25–27 inches for a female

Weight: 88–99 pounds for a male, 70.5–77 pounds for a female

Color: black and dark brown with reddish brown markings

The short coat is easy to care for but offers no protection against cold, dampness, and heat.

Born in 1834 in Apolda, Germany, Louis Dobermann was a dogcatcher, tax collector, night policeman, and animal furrier. He bred his dogs to be unconditional fighters, incorruptible guard dogs, and aggressive toward intruders and people in general; these dogs were not frightened by gunshots. This outspoken, one-person dog will only respect the person he deems as a leader. He is very territorial and intolerant of strange dogs and people. Early socialization with other dogs and people will prevent him from biting or fighting. Doberman owners who do not want a well-socialized dog and encourage his innate aggressiveness have given this dog a bad reputation. He is easy to care for and very spirited; he needs plenty of exercise and meaningful tasks. He is ever vigilant and always in an attentive position. He barks readily, and his prey drive must be kept under control by consistent training. A good Doberman is never afraid, nervous, or aggressive without cause. The Doberman must be well trained. He enjoys dog sports. This breed is recognized as a service breed and is not for people who lead an inactive lifestyle. He should never be acquired on an impulse.

111

Archetypal Dogs

Left: Siberian huskies are the racehorses among the sled dogs.

Right: The Czechoslovakian wolfhound is a mix of wolf and dog.

Far right: Keeshonds are territorial.

Bottom: A small, charming hunter, the Shiba Inu is from Japan.

Archetypal dogs are called that because their appearance and their relationship with people have not changed for thousands of years, proven by ancient rock engravings known as petroglyphs. Humans have not bred them to change them in any way but rather to make use of their versatile capabilities. These dogs typically have pointed, erect ears and a tail that curls upward and lies against the back. These archetypal dogs are used as sled dogs, hunting dogs, herding dogs, and watchdogs. Some breeds are still used for these purposes today, some have adapted to the requirements of changing circumstances, and some have only recently been created by crossbreeding. They have a completely instinctive predisposition, are strongly socially oriented pack hunters, and, with the exception of sled dogs, are very territorial. These breeds are fascinating; they have preserved their independence and are therefore not very easy to keep in our modern society. They are not cozy companions. The exception to this is the German spitz, which has lived in a domestic setting for many centuries and has adapted accordingly to our civilized society.

› Sled Dogs

From the beginning of the human-dog relationship, nomadic hunters took advantage of the husky's ability as a sled dog. This form of transportation was used to make the journey to and from the communal hunt, to carry back the prey, or to transport belongings from one place to another. Depending on habitat, some huskies were used to protect grazing stock. Their relationship with humans was mutually useful because life for both people and animals was tough. They shared common tasks for mutual benefit but lived in separate worlds.

It is in a young dog's nature to learn by watching and imitating, so the effort required to train these dogs was minimal. Those that did not follow the rules could put the community at risk and therefore would not survive. Being bound to just

one person was undesirable because the dog had to work with anyone who needed him. These dogs have preserved their independence even today. Hunting is in their blood, and the ranking order of the pack is vital to them; however, being subordinate without a very good reason makes no sense to them. They need a lot of space and are in no way suited to living in an apartment. Traditional training methods are a complete failure with this type of dog. Rather, you have to earn their respect as a pack leader, which is much more difficult than it sounds!

> Hunting Dogs

The three Laika breeds fall under FCI's Nordic Hunting Dogs category. They are also known as Russian spitz. The Japanese spitz has many fans worldwide. The dogs look very pretty, but they are difficult; as independent hunters that forage and flush, they do things of their

own accord and will only be subordinate to a very strong pack leader. Because people no longer tend to hunt, in the dog's eyes, the human is a failure. This means that the dog will try to dominate when outdoors. These dogs are alert

and defend their territory, so they are intolerant of other dogs. The African basenji is also an archetypal hunting dog but lives in a very different habitat.

> Herding Dogs

The archetypal herder is the Icelandic sheepdog, which became a friend of humankind.

> Watchdogs

European breeds are more clingy and willing to submit than Asian breeds. They were used as rat and mice catchers and were kept outside the house, most likely on the manure pile, and reported on everything that went by. They are intolerant of strangers even today. The primitive archetypal watchdog was the basis of breeds such as the German shepherd, which has the sharp senses of a wolf but has adapted to fit in to life with humans.

Siberian Husky and Alaskan Malamute

Siberian Husky

Shoulder height: 21–23.5 inches for a male, 20–22 inches for s female

Weight: 45–62 pounds for a male, 34–51 pounds for a female

Color: pure white to red and black with all colors in between, typically white mask

Alaskan Malamute

Shoulder height: 25 inches for a male, 23 inches for a female

Weight: 84 pounds for a male, 75 pounds for a female

Color: all shades from wolf gray to black and from sand to red with lighter or pure white markings

Alaskan huskies are hybrids bred purely for racing.

Siberian Husky

This is a breed kept by nomadic reindeer herders, fishermen, and hunters in Siberia. In 1909, a Russian fur trader brought the first huskies to Alaska where they performed successfully in sled dog races. They became famous for their participation in relay races, which were around 674 miles long. They transported serum used to treat diphtheria and rescued the city of Nome from an epidemic. Huskies have strong hunting instincts, are masters of escape, are never willing to submit, and are conceivably unsuitable as pets, even though they are lovable and not aggressive toward humans and dogs.

Alaskan Malamute

The dog of the Malamutes, a tribe in western Alaska, became famous for pulling sleds in polar expeditions. This muscular dog has a pronounced self-confidence, is never willing to submit, and needs consistent training from the start. He is not a dog for beginners, nor for people who neither have the time nor the inclination to work intensively with the dog in order to train him thoroughly. He is a working dog that can be used for sled sports, Nordic skiing, and racing. The malamute is vigilant and very athletic.

Both breeds need a strong leader, meaningful tasks, plenty of space, and cannot be kept in the house or apartment.

Top: a Siberian husky

Right: an Alaskan malamute

Samoyed and Greenland Dog

Samoyed

Shoulder height: 22.5 inches for a male, 21 inches for a female

Weight: 45–65 pounds for a male, 35–50 pounds for a female

Color: pure white, cream, or white with biscuit

Greenland Dog

Shoulder height: minimum 23.5 for a male, 21.5 for a female

Weight: 66–70 pounds

Color: all except albinos

Greenland dogs were used for hunting polar bears and seals.

Top: a Samoyed

Below: a Greenland dog

Samoyed

This dog was bred to be a hunter, reindeer herder, and sled dog for the Samoyed, a Russian tribe. He had a close bond with humans and was allowed to live in the tents; however, his independence was never disputed. The Samoyed is intelligent, attentive, energetic, and loves human affection. He must be kept busy and needs plenty of exercise. Rugged and weatherproof, he loves to be outdoors. He is not happy to submit and needs consistent leadership; his passion for hunting and freedom means he will go his own way. As a sled dog he is more determined than he is fast. His white coat is maintenance intensive. He is always happy and charming but despite this, he is not an easy dog to own.

Greenland Dog

Most of all the original sled dog breeds from Greenland are still used for traditional work. Purely a tool for the Inuits, he spends his life in his harness and has no close bond with his people. The dogs cooperate with people in the hard struggle for survival, assisting with hunting and sled pulling. They are aggressive toward other dogs and are not suited to life in our modern world.

115

Medium German Spitz and Miniature German Spitz

Medium German Spitz

Shoulder height: 12–15 inches

Weight: 23–41 pounds

Color: black, white, brown, orange, gray, cream, cream sable, orange sable, black and tan, pintos

Miniature German Spitz

Shoulder height: 9–11.5 inches

Weight: 18–22 pounds

Color: same as the medium German spitz

The medium German spitz is one of the most endangered dog breeds.

Spitz dogs are the oldest domesticated dogs of all, and the breed was developed all over the world. In particular, the German spitz is an excellent home and family dog and was formerly a part of people's daily lives. They were appreciated for their vigilance and zest for life and as rat and mice catchers.

This image as an ordinary, archetypal dog has meant he has fallen behind newer, more prestigious breeds. The medium spitz and the miniature spitz are very adaptable and also suitable as apartment dogs. With appropriate training, the dog's readiness to bark can be kept under control, but the spitz is always a reliable guard dog that is suspicious of strangers. He is devoted to his people, sensitive, and loves to exercise. He is large enough to take part in long hikes but small enough to be taken everywhere with his owner. This very docile dog is easy to train and is characterized by his lack of hunting instinct and his affectionate nature. Spitz dogs are easy to care for. The long fur needs regular care but does not tend to become matted.

Giant German Spitz and Keeshond

Giant German Spitz
Shoulder height: 16.5–19.5 inches
Weight: 38.5–40 pounds
Color: black, white, brown

Keeshond
Shoulder height: 17–21.5 inches
Weight: 35–45 pounds
Color: silver gray with black fur-tips, black muzzle

The giant German spitz is another breed threatened with extinction.

Previous page, top: a miniature German spitz

Previous page, bottom: a medium German spitz

Top and bottom right: the Keeshond

Bottom left: a giant German spitz

Giant German Spitz

The giant spitz is not actually all that giant—he is considered a medium-sized dog. His ancestors are the Nordic herding dogs, such as the Samoyed. According to some historical accounts, the Vikings brought these dogs to Germany. Very vigilant and territorial, he makes an ideal watchdog for the farm or country house. The spitz has a confident personality and is reluctant to submit. He loves walks, being outdoors, and working as a guard dog. He tolerates strange dogs, albeit reluctantly. He is an attractive companion dog.

Keeshond

This breed, also known as the wolfspitz, is an old farm watchdog breed. This proud personality commands attention and respect. He is an incorruptible guard dog with an innate protective instinct. No intruder would survive unscathed. However, he is not willing to be subordinate and must be trained using plenty of patience, empathy, and consistency. The robust Keeshond loves being outdoors and needs plenty of exercise and meaningful tasks. Because of his low propensity for poaching, he can be happily kept as a watchdog in an area that is rich in wildlife. As a distinctly territorial dog, he is not friendly toward other dogs.

117

Schipperke

Shoulder height: 10–13 inches

Weight: 6.5–20 pounds

Color: black

This breed loves to work and is very cooperative, so he is well suited to agility training.

This little spitz sheepdog derives his name from the Flemish word *scheperke* meaning "small shepherd." He was mentioned in fifteenth-century writings and was depicted in many paintings of peasant life by old Flemish masters. He was used for herding but more often for rat catching on farms and also as a watchdog. Flemish sailors also used him on ships, and, even today, he can still be found working on large barges, which earned him the nickname "Little Captain." He became a favorite pet of the Belgian Queen Marie Henriette in the nineteenth century. He is lively, inquisitive, attentive, and an incorruptible guard dog that will passionately defend his territory. This little black creature will bark and defend without causing anyone serious injury. He is intelligent and docile, full of spirit, ideal to keep in the home, and he enjoys a close bond with his people. He is not friendly toward strangers and sometimes even intolerant of them. The schipperke loves to work with horses. His short fur is easy to care for.

Czechoslovakian Wolfdog and Saarloos Wolfdog

Czechoslovakian Wolfdog

Shoulder height: minimum 25.5 for a male, minimum 23.5 for a female

Weight: minimum 57 pounds for a male, minimum 44 pounds for a female

Color: yellow gray, wolf gray, and silver gray

Saarloos Wolfdog

Shoulder height: 25.5-29.5 inches for a male, 23.5–27.5 inches for a female

Weight: 79–90 pounds

Color: brown and gray wolf colors, light cream to white

Both breeds need owners with plenty of knowledge about canine behavior.

Over thousands of years, people have bred the wolf to become a domestic dog. Wolf hybrids are seen as a rather questionable experiment. The innate wolf behavior must be kept under control with very early training. Puppies must be socialized from the start in order to get used to our environment without suffering stress because they are innately suspicious of all strangers. They require a secure enclosure because they are masters of escape. Owners must have an in-depth knowledge of wolf and dog behavior and a lot of time and empathy. Wolfdogs are highly intelligent, with sharper senses and faster reactions than dogs. The wolf's entire repertoire of instinctive behavior, including social behavior, is fully evident, and he has a pronounced passion for hunting. All in all, this is a difficult animal to keep. Leendert Saarloos from Holland wanted to combine the sharp senses of the wolf with the German shepherd's willingness to learn and his strong bond with humans. Saarloos wanted to create the perfect guide dog for the blind, but unfortunately, he was not successful. Saarloos wolfdogs have a strong tendency to stray. The Czechoslovakian wolfdog is also a wolf and German shepherd cross and was bred for the military as a service dog. He is persistent, spirited, and docile but not subservient.

Top: a Czechoslovakian wolfdog

Left: a Saarloos wolfdog

119

Chow Chow

Shoulder height: 19–22 inches for a male, 18–20 inches for a female

Weight: 45–70 pounds

Color: solid black, red, blue, fawn, cream, and white

The thick long fur must be carefully maintained; otherwise, this breed can suffer from eczema.

Top: a long-haired chow chow

Below: short-haired chow chows

Mongols brought chow chows with them to China as hunting, guard, and war dogs. Ancient terracotta figures and paintings depict the heavier spitz type. The first chow chows arrived in England about one hundred years ago. *Chao chao* means "all-seeing," "alert," and "clever," and is a perfect description of the characteristics of this dog. The chow chow has a strong, self-confident personality. Chow chows are reserved with strangers, very vigilant, but do not tend to bark. This breed is devoted to its people, but never submissive. He will only follow the one who has proved himself to be a loving and unique pack leader, which is why he is known as a one-person dog. The chow chow is not keen on running but loves his walks. Due to his pronounced hunting instinct, he can only be let off the leash in areas free of wildlife. His hind legs are much longer than his front legs, and his stilted gait is not suited to dog sports. If you are planning to purchase one of these dogs, make sure you pick a healthy specimen with black eye rims and eyelids, which neither turn in nor droop. The pupils of the eyes should be clearly visible. The short-haired chow was bred from the original Chinese imported breed.

Shar-Pei

Shoulder height: 17–20 inches

Weight: 40–55 pounds

Color: all solid colors except white

The so-called miniature shar-peis are bred in the United States but are not yet an officially recognized breed.

This ancient Chinese breed was bred to hunt wild boar and was kept as a herding, farm, and house dog. In the 1950s, these dogs nearly became extinct in China, but a few shar-peis managed to survive in Taiwan, Macao, and Hong Kong. In 1971, breeder Matgo Law asked an American newspaper for help with the preservation of the breed. The mission was a success: puppy prices rose to dizzying heights and the shar-pei became a status symbol in the United States. Only the puppies were exhibited as show dogs because they have the characteristic wrinkles; the adults less so. Extreme wrinkling in the adult dog is due to a hormonal imbalance; it causes skin problems and also menstrual disorders in females and is undesirable. Eyes that are too deep set and small cause eyelids to curl, resulting in painful inflammations. Apart from these excesses, which responsible breeders do not support, the shar-pei is a unique, spirited, cheerful, and affectionate yet quiet pet. Aloof with strangers, he is alert and watchful but not aggressive. He is a very clean dog and can be kept in an apartment.

Eurasier

Shoulder height: 20.5–23.5 inches for a male, 19–22 inches for a female

Weight: 51–70.5 pounds for a male, 39.5–57 for a female

Color: all except white, with colored blotches, or liver

The Eurasier was officially recognized in 1973.

Julius Wipfel bred the Eurasier in the 1960s as a successor to his wolf-chow, a cross between the Keeshond and the chow chow. Later came the Samoyed. He was aiming for a sociable, healthy breed with a natural elegance and friendly nature. In 1973, the breed was officially recognized. The Eurasier is a pleasant, quiet house dog, with pronounced social behavior and a good dose of stubbornness. Eurasiers love to learn all their lives. The confident companion appreciates meaningful tasks and plenty of exercise. He is affectionate and sensitive. As a territorial and confident dog, he is alert and always ready to defend. Occasionally the Samoyed in him emerges, shown by his passion for hunting; this must be kept under control with good training. The Eurasier is not a breed for beginners. It is essential that an owner has a very good knowledge of canine behavior in order to be an effective pack leader for this dog. The dense fur is relatively easy to care for but must be brushed intensively during the shedding season. Breed clubs enforce strict breeding controls to ensure healthy dogs and to prevent commercialization of this breed.

Akita Inu, Shiba Inu, and American Akita

Akita Inu and American Akita

The companion of the Samurai has become a part of Japanese mythology. Akitas are viewed as lucky. These dogs hunted bears and antelopes and were excellent watchdogs. The first Akitas arrived in the United States in 1937; American soldiers brought them home after World War II as presents, and then bred them. The American type is bigger, more solid, and more colorful. In 1998, the Akitas were separated into two breeds. She is very territorial, mistrustful of strangers, and aggressive toward other dogs. These large, strong dogs are not for beginners; they require an owner with a lot of understanding and patience to deal with their unique characteristics. A securely enclosed area of land is required.

Shiba Inu

The Shiba Inu is an ancient hunting dog of small animals and birds, as well as bears and wild boar. She is an intelligent, funny housemate; however, she is also very confident, independent, and has a pronounced passion for hunting. She is not a dog for beginners; she needs to be constantly reminded who is pack leader.

Akita Inu (left)
Shoulder height: 25–27.5 inches for a male, 23–25 inches for a female

Weight: 75–120 pounds for a male, 75–110 for a female

Color: red, white, brindle, sesame

Shiba Inu
(bottom right)
Shoulder height: 16 inches for a male, 14.5 inches for a female

Weight: 18–25 pounds for a male, 15–20 pounds for a female

Color: red, black and tan, sesame, black sesame, red sesame

American Akita
(bottom left)
Shoulder height: 26–28 inches for a male, 24–26 inches for a female

Weight: 75–120 pounds for a male, 75–110 pounds for a female

Color: any color including white, blotched, or spotted

It is not a good idea to let these passionate hunters off the leash.

Basenji

Shoulder height: 17 inches for a male, 16 inches for a female

Weight: 24 pounds for a male, 21 pounds for a female

Color: black and white, red and white, brindle, black and tan

The basenji's short fur is practical and easy to care for.

This breed is a primitive domestic dog that resides in slums and developed areas in the tropics; she lives alongside humans but has to fend for herself. The basenji from the Congo is the only type that has been officially recognized. The aborigines regard her as an indispensable hunting assistant; she forages and flushes and is cared for by the tribes in return. She has an excellent nose. Explorers of the nineteenth century brought the first examples to England, where they were purebred. The basenji has an unusual bark; she expresses her emotions with a brief woof, which is either a deep rumble or a yodel. She is easy to care for, but she is not for everyone. Severity makes her shy, stubborn, and disobedient. She is indifferent to strangers. The docile, ever-cheerful, playful dog needs to be treated with love and understanding; as an independent hunter, being subordinate does not come naturally to her. Her hunting instinct is stronger than her bond with people. If there are no areas where you can let her off her leash, you will have to provide her with lots of space, plenty of exercise, and meaningful tasks. If underutilized, she will seek her own entertainment that will rarely be to the liking of her owner. Her short coat offers no protection against heat, cold, or dampness. As long as she keeps moving, the winter weather will not bother her. She especially treasures a cozy couch indoors!

Icelandic Sheepdog

Shoulder height: ideal 18 inches for a male, ideal 16.5 inches for a female

Weight: 25–45 pounds for a male, 20–40 pounds for a female

Coat: short-haired and long-haired varieties

Color: any shade from cream to reddish brown, chocolate brown, gray, black; white always present but never dominant (more than 50 percent)

The only Icelandic dog breed arrived on the island with Viking settlers.

This age-old former hunting breed from Iceland was soon assigned the task of sheepdog due to the lack of available wildlife to hunt. Although she collaborated closely with people, she was never kept as a family dog in the home. Rigorous selection for performance and health made the Icelandic sheepdog a robust, undemanding, obedient, agile, courageous dog that loves to work and is undeterred by rough terrain or bad weather. The benign, friendly Icelandic dog loves to have a close bond with her people, and she learns quickly and willingly. She is sensitive, and therefore must be consistently trained without severity. The Icelandic dog is alert, but she does not bite. Aggressive dogs were never tolerated in this breed. She tolerates other dogs and animals well. The lively breed barks readily and needs plenty of exercise and meaningful tasks. She is a wonderful horse-riding companion; she feels quite at home in paddocks and stables. She is not an apartment dog, nor is she for people with an inactive lifestyle. This breed's appearance varies quite a bit; there are long-haired and short-haired varieties, and their fur comes in a wide range of colors. The dense fur is easy to care for.

Boar, Bear, and Bull Baiters

Left: The boxer is a fun-loving, affectionate housemate.

Right: The Dogue de Bordeaux exudes serenity.

Bottom: The Dogo Canario from the Canary Island of El Hierro is a reliable watchdog.

Unarmed, a human could barely catch a mouse, let alone kill a large animal. Hunter-gatherers who collected fruits and berries needed the help of dogs to hunt large prey. People hunted large game in densely wooded areas. Agile dogs weakened the wild boar or rounded up the bear; the strong boar and bear baiters made repeated attacks on the game until the hunter dared to get close enough to move in for the kill. Reliable, experienced dogs saved lives and livelihoods. Hunting scenes, which glorify the courage of the animal and human but also show such cruelty, can be found in many writings and accounts from the eighteenth century. Around this time, the use of traditional hunting methods began to fall out of favor due to continuous improvements made to guns. Eventually dangerous species were no longer hunted using traditional methods.

In ancient times, these dogs hunted the big game of the Orient and Africa. In wars, they fought on the front lines, protected by armor. The Spanish conquerors of South America set their dogs on the natives. The cruelty of the human race manifests itself in the way humans use their dogs. When these dogs were no longer required to hunt bears and wild boar, they found new careers as courageous watchdogs and guard dogs. Slaughterers used them to bait bulls.

The adrenaline rush of tortured animals made meat more edible for humans. To this day, unscrupulous people use dogs that will fight to

the bitter end for the sake of entertainment. Specialized breeds were bred for animal fighting, and although this was later outlawed, it carried on illegally. In the United States a "dog fight scene" developed and spilled over into Europe, where it is now a well-known phenomenon. Because the descendants of boar-charging breeds are not agile or aggressive enough for fighting, they were crossed with hot-blooded terriers. This created a merciless breed that does not stop until it has finished the job. In private, these dogs are very affectionate because aggression

against people was never a desirable trait. But when such dogs feel the need to bite, they will do so; they know no pain and no going back.

Today some excellent family dogs can be found among the former boar-charging breeds, and these dogs are not aggressive unless provoked. They are not easily provoked, however, and prefer to use threatening behavior rather than actually biting, unless they are in real danger. Their physical superiority in both their strength and their willingness to fight the enemy is accompanied by a dominant nature. They are not stupid and perfectly able to learn, but why obey when it makes no sense? They are usually passively dominant and apply various tactics to assert themselves such as stubbornness, ignorance, and buffoonery. As is typical of strongly territorial dogs, they are reserved toward strangers, make reliable guard dogs, and are often intolerant of strange dogs. However, in strange territory, they behave in a neutral manner. With the exception of the very energetic, spirited boxer, walks are usually taken at an even pace, and they have a limited need for exercise. One exception is the Fila Brasileiro, which is a powerful hunter. She needs her own area to roam and guard. These breeds are the grown-ups of the dog world and take their role as guard dog very seriously. They do not need to be entertained with fun and games. For young dogs, games where they can assert their dominance should be avoided.

127

Great Dane

Shoulder height: minimum
31.5 inches for a male,
minimum 28 inches for
a female

Weight: 120–200 pounds
for a male, 100–130
pounds for a female

Color: yellow, brindle,
black, blue, black and
white flecked

**Improper rearing of this
giant breed can lead to
severe skeletal damage.**

These so-called royal hounds lived privileged lives; they were the embodiment of strength, pride, and nobility. In the nineteenth century, this breed was kept in the houses of wealthy citizens, was one of the first breeds to be bred according to standard, and won a high number of awards at some of the very first dog shows. Irresponsible breeding leads to overly large dogs with deformities, health problems, and a lower life expectancy. Because she is such a powerful and spirited dog, achieving the right character is of the utmost importance. The Great Dane is gentle, good natured, and must be trained lovingly and consistently from puppyhood by someone with a good knowledge of canine behavior. She must learn to obey her owner's word and should never be frightening or aggressive. Nevertheless, this giant breed has a strong personality, and it is not easy for a person to qualify as pack leader in her eyes. She is sovereign and benign, however, and she is quite forgiving of any weaknesses in her owner. She needs a lot of space, loves to be close to her family, and loves her walks. The Great Dane makes a reliable guard dog; after all, who would want to put this dog's threats to the test? Rearing one of these dogs is time consuming and expensive, due to her enormous size.

Boxer

Shoulder height: 22.5–25 inches for a male, 21–23 inches for a female

Weight: 66 pounds and up for a male, about 55 pounds for a female

Color: fawn and brindle, with or without white markings

The boxer is a well-known service dog breed.

This former boar charger was kept by butchers and cattle dealers. Her broad muzzle and short nose allowed her to grab and hold on to her prey without suffocation. The breed name first came about in 1860 and pure breeding began in Munich, Germany. The friendly, charming family dog is an incorruptible guard dog that never barks unnecessarily. She is always ready to play and run and is never touchy. She can be easily trained with loving consistency, but she does need repetition because she is stubborn and will sometimes clown around in an attempt to dominate you. You can put her in her place without needing to be overly severe, but be careful not to get drawn in by her cute facial expressions! An owner who has managed to successfully train and motivate his boxer will find her to be an excellent companion for dog sports. This spirited breed needs plenty of exercise and meaningful tasks, and a close family bond is essential. As long as these basic requirements are met, she is an excellent housemate that will appreciate the luxury of a soft sofa. Her short coat is easy to care for; however, she is sensitive to cold and heat. Cold and rain will not upset her as long as she keeps moving. She is prone to heat stroke. White puppies are occasionally born in a litter, and although they are not permitted according to the standard, they have plenty of fans.

Bulldog and Bullmastiff

Bulldog

Shoulder height: 12–16 inches

Weight: 55 pounds for a male, 50 pounds for a female

Color: all colors except gray, black, and black and tan

Bullmastiff

Shoulder height: 25–27 inches for a male, 24–26 inches for a female

Weight: 110–130 pounds for a male, 90–110 pounds for a female

Color: brindle, red and light brown, dark mask

A bullmastiff will usually tolerate a dog of the opposite gender but will act aggressively toward a dog of the same gender, no matter the size or breed.

Bulldog

Bull baiting was a popular "sport" for centuries in England, and people from all classes wagered large sums of money at events. The ideal bulldog was stocky, short legged, and immensely steadfast with an enormously strong neck and powerful jaw. The short nose and strength of the protruding lower jaw allowed her to grab and hold onto her prey without being suffocated. The muscular dog with lightning-fast reactions was unfortunately bred irresponsibly and found breathing and movement difficult. However, when responsibly bred, she is a cheerful, friendly family dog that is also enchanting, charming, and obstinate. Because of her anatomy and shortness of breath, she has little need for exercise.

Bullmastiff

This breed is the result of a cross between a mastiff and a bulldog. As a guard dog belonging to gamekeepers, she grabs and keeps hold of poachers but does not actually bite them. She is also a popular watchdog for large properties. The strong, lively dog with the ferocious face is a loyal, trustworthy companion with a balanced nature. She should never be aggressive or fearful. She is not keen on running and does not stray. She can learn obedience by being trained lovingly but does not submit willingly.

Top: a bulldog

Right: a bullmastiff

Dogue de Bordeaux and Mastiff

Dogue de Bordeaux

Shoulder height: 23.5–27 inches for a male, 23–26 inches for a female

Weight: minimum 110 pounds for a male, minimum 99 pounds for a female

Color: reddish brown with brown or black mask

Mastiff

Shoulder height: minimum 30 inches for a male, minimum 27 inches for a female

Weight: 160 pounds for a male, 150 pounds for a female

Color: apricot brown, silver brown, fawn brown, or dark brown brindle, black mask

Great care must be taken when rearing, feeding, and exercising puppies.

Dogue de Bordeaux

An old boar-charger breed that originated in France, she was also kept as a watchdog, guard dog, and butcher's dog in Bordeaux. She is a quiet, well-balanced family dog that is tolerant of strangers. She is sensitive and needs consistent, loving training. Properly trained, this dog is obedient and not prone to straying or hunting. She does not have a pronounced love of running, but she needs freedom of movement and her own space. A Dogue de Bordeaux starred alongside Tom Hanks in the 1989 movie *Turner and Hooch*, which was about a police officer and his dog.

Mastiff

When the Romans arrived in Britain, they admired this giant dog and took her to Rome to fight in the bullfighting arenas. This ancient breed is solid and strong. She is a hunting and guard dog that became almost extinct during both world wars. The breed was built back up by a crossing with the Great Dane, bullmastiff, and Newfoundland, among others. The mastiff is friendly and good natured. She should never be fearful or aggressive. This sensitive giant must be brought up with love and firmness; she is quietly dominant and will never be completely subordinate.

Top: a Dogue de Bordeaux

Left: a mastiff

131

Bull Terrier, Staffordshire Bull Terrier, and American Staffordshire Terrier

Bull Terrier (right)
Shoulder height: 20–24 inches
Weight: 45–80 pounds
Color: white, black brindle, red, fawn, and tricolor; with colored dogs, one color must be predominant

Staffordshire Bull Terrier (bottom left)
Shoulder height: 14–16 inches
Weight: 28–37.5 pounds for a male, 24–34 pounds for a female
Color: red, fawn, white, black, blue, brindle with or without white

American Staffordshire Terrier (bottom right)
Shoulder height: 18–19 inches for a male, 17–18 inches for a female
Weight: 57–67 pounds
Color: all colors, solid, bicolored, or patched, but patterned coats must be predominantly white; black and tan and liver colors are undesirable

All three breeds often appear on dangerous dogs and banned breeds lists.

Several local governments in different states have made it illegal to own these breeds. Therefore, before purchasing one of these dogs, check which conditions apply according to where you live to ensure you do not break the law. The English bull terrier is a result of crossing aggressive terrier breeds with bulldogs and was bred specifically for animal fighting. The Staffordshire bull terrier breed has evolved over the years to become a popular family dog in England. In the nineteenth century, these dogs were brought to the United States where they were pure bred. In the United States, illegal dog fighting became popular, which then spilled over into Europe. These terriers are self-confident, unwilling to submit, and will not go out of their way to avoid a fight; they will fight to the death.

Fila Brasileiro

Shoulder height: 25.5–29.5 inches for a male, 23.5–27.5 inches for a female

Weight: minimum 110 pounds for a male, minimum 88 pounds for a female

Color: all except pure white, mouse gray, black and tan, blue, or more than one-quarter white

When purchasing a puppy, it is essential to make sure it has been reared in close contact with humans!

Here is the original boar baiter; still today, this breed is bred to hunt large game, even jaguars. The coveted watchdogs and guard dogs preside over large properties. These energetic herders originate from breeds in Spain and Portugal. Later, the breed was crossed with European breeds such as the mastiff and bloodhounds. Filas have a natural distrust of strangers. Her protective instinct and readiness to defend are innate and cannot be trained out of her. Her character is of crucial importance as is the socialization of the puppies if they are to become good family dogs. When among her family, she is a loyal and even affectionate pet. Fila owners must have experience with dogs and a sound knowledge of canine behavior. Traditional training methods and repetition bore her. Great care must be taken with training, rearing, exercise, and diet. This impressive Brazilian dog needs a close family connection, but she must learn to accept her place in the pack because this will not come naturally to her. She is not a dog for those with inactive lifestyles; she is very spirited, needs plenty of exercise, and is an avid hunter.

Companion Dogs

Left: Boston terriers are always cheerful.

Below: The Chihuahua may be the smallest dog in the world, but she has a huge personality.

These breeds have the dubious pleasure of being bred solely for the enjoyment of people. Dogs with particular mutations were bred to produce cute little pets. Humans treasured these freaks of nature and knew how to make the most of these different mutations. These little dogs were not only reared for enjoyment, but they also gave humans much affection. It has now been scientifically proven that petting a dog has a soothing effect on the heart and circulatory system, not to mention the soul. Those who look contemptuously at small dogs soon change their mind once they come into contact with such a creature; what she lacks in size, she makes up for in personality. Nothing beats the pleasant feeling of a little dog stretching out her body and burrowing her head into your neck for a snooze. These small, clever dogs with sweet faces are full of tenderness and devotion and can often make up for what we are missing in our human relationships. Many of these little breeds need experienced owners who can understand their unique ways.

The mutations and characteristics of the early miniature dog breeds barely resemble today's modern breeds, if at all. Selective breeding aimed to produce dogs that had youthful behavior well into old age, a willingness to be subordinate, and a very close attachment to the caregiver. Other than a few exceptions, these dogs are playful as adults, easy to train, devoted, obedient, and have no inclination to stray.

Among these breeds we find some of the more high-maintenance dogs. Many people have an innate need to care for vulnerable animals; however, a few of these breeds were cursed with an excessive amount of fur for show dog purposes. They may be successful at dog shows, but often they are prevented from leading the normal life of a dog. The same goes for dogs with very squashed faces; their quality of life is impaired by breathing difficulties, not to mention complications when birthing.

⟩ Bichons

Little white lap dogs were found in Mediterranean countries in ancient times. Bichons are characterized by their irresistible charm and cheerful vitality. However, they need intensive grooming. If you do not wish to exhibit your dog, the fur can be trimmed so it is easier to maintain.

⟩ Small Terriers

These silky-haired terriers are less independent and more sociable than the typical terrier. The mini bull terrier does not deny her true bull terrier heritage, but her smaller size makes her a lot easier to handle.

⟩ Schnauzers, Pinschers, and Spitz

The smallest examples of the former house and farm dogs lived a life of luxury in close proximity to humans. They exhibit the courageous behavior of their ancestors, but they are not as independent.

⟩ Small Mastiffs

Their snub noses, round heads, and large eyes appeal to our innate instincts; we as humans are programmed to care for infants with such features. Unfortunately, irresponsible breeding led to extremes.

⟩ Asian Breeds

These dogs were bred to represent the image of the lion, which was said to be able to transform into the Buddha himself when in danger. They were well cared for in palaces and monasteries. In China, pets were bred that could not survive without human intervention; the Pekingese is an example of this. However, European breeders followed this trend and further emphasized the characteristics of these breeds.

⟩ Gundogs

Here we find the descendants of the flushing dogs—gundogs with handlers. They are prepared to submit, and their attachment outweighs their hunting instinct, if any such instinct exists at all. The Kromfohrländer (Krom dog) is an exception: she is a descendant of independent hunting dogs but is specifically bred to be a companion dog.

⟩ Exotics

Hairless dogs from Asia, Africa, and South America served as a source of warmth, medicine, and food. Hairlessness is a recessive gene and is accompanied by the loss of teeth. The quality of life, however, is not impaired.

Poodle and Romagna Water Dog

Poodle

Shoulder height: *Standard:* 18–23.5 inches, *Medium:* 14–18 inches, *Miniature:* 11–14 inches, *Toy:* 9.5–11 inches

Weight: *Standard:* 45–70 pounds, *Medium:* 20–30 pounds, *Miniature:* 15–17 pounds, *Toy:* 6–9 pounds

Coat: curly and corded (very rare)

Color: solid black, white, brown, gray, apricot

Romagna Water Dog

Shoulder height: 17–19 inches for a male, 16–18 inches for a female

Weight: 28.5–35 pounds for a male, 24–31 pounds for a female

Color: solid off-white, white with brown or orange patches, brown roan, brown with or without white, orange with or without white

One great advantage of both these breeds is that neither of them sheds.

Top: an apricot standard poodle

Right: a Romagna water dog

Poodle

Poodle breeds were the companions of noble ladies in ancient times. They were very popular in the baroque era (1600s) and rococo era (1700s). These descendants of the ancient water dog were the basis for many hunting breeds. The poodle is intelligent, very affectionate toward her people, playful into old age, and easily trainable with few behavioral problems. The curly coat should be shorn about every eight weeks and must be brushed daily. Owners who do not want to exhibit their dogs can keep the hairstyle elegantly short; this gives her a noble appearance, particularly for the large poodle. The poodle is vigilant but not aggressive and is not a barker. She is neutral with strangers. She loves long walks and is compatible with other dogs. The standard poodle is ideal for dog sports. She occasionally exhibits hunting tendencies.

Romagna Water Dog

This was an ancient breed from Italy, where she was once kept as a truffle-sniffing dog. She is eager to learn, eager to work, affectionate, and easy to train. She is suitable for all kinds of dog sports. The tousled, insulating, curly coat is short over the entire body.

Yorkshire Terrier and Australian Silky Terrier

Yorkshire Terrier

Many terrier breeds and the Maltese dog contributed to the development of this breed.

The Yorkie is of a happy disposition and has astonishing wisdom and adaptability. An ideal companion for the smallest living space in the city, she likes her walks. The elaborate floor-length coat of a show dog needs a lot of care; it is oiled and wrapped in tissue paper for protection. For domestic purposes and also the well-being of the dog, the fur can be trimmed short. Do not buy puppies that have been kept in cages or bred by traders.

Australian Silky Terrier

British immigrants brought their terriers with them to Australia. The steel-blue wire-haired Yorkshire terrier was mated with the Dandie Dinmont, which resulted in a similar variant. The silky is a happy, uncomplicated breed that loves to exercise. She is intelligent and easily trainable. She is still, according to her standard, a rat catcher, so her terrier image has been preserved. As long as she is exercised properly, she is a perfect apartment dog. The coat needs care, but the length of the fur is not bred to a set standard.

French Bulldog

Shoulder height: 12 inches

Weight: 17.5–31 pounds

Color: fawn, brindle, or white with brindle patches

The eye and nose folds must be kept clean; this breed is otherwise easy to care for.

British settlers in Normandy, France, brought their miniature bulldogs over with them. Although the breed fell out of favor in the United Kingdom, it flourished in France, particularly in Paris. There they were crossed with terriers and griffons to create a small bulldog breed that was considerably different from the English bulldog in both temperament and appearance. The French bulldog became more socially acceptable and even downright fashionable when the English king, Edward VII, acquired one. Unfortunately, because of the dog's physical proportions (big head and narrow pelvis), this breed has birthing problems. Many dogs suffer from shortness of breath, snore, and are sensitive to heat. The bully is intelligent, kind, affectionate, and cuddly. This lively dog ready to share the joy and sorr He likes to walk, b attentive The Fren and parti for the eld adaptable a content in a lively family.

Boston Terrier

Shoulder height: about 14–16.5 inches

Weight: *Light:* up to 15 pounds, *Medium:* 15–20 pounds, *Heavy:* 20–25 pounds; females are usually somewhat lighter

Color: brindle, black, or seal with white markings

The tail is naturally short or stubby.

The Boston terrier, as the name suggests, was created in Boston, Massachusetts; he is a result of a crossing between the English bulldog and a white English terrier. He was also later crossed with a French bulldog. This adaptable dog is always cheerful, loves fun and games, and is extremely people oriented. He requires very little training because he is very intelligent, sensitive, and highly responsive to his owner's voice. The extraordinarily affectionate Boston is alert but not a barker; however, he will defend his territory furiously against strangers. Despite his history of pure breeding, there is sometimes more bulldog heritage than any other; this manifests itself both in his nature and also his solid build. The majority of the lighter build types are always ready to play. The little powerhouse has plenty of confidence and loves to run. The fine coat is easy to maintain. He is an ideal city and apartment dog for people who want to take their dog everywhere with them and those who appreciate a fun-loving companion; there is never a dull moment with the Boston terrier! One distinctive characteristic of the Boston is his intelligent expression, marked by his large, deep, dark eyes and his permanently pricked-up ears.

139

Pug and Petit Brabançon

Pug (right)

Shoulder height: 10–14 inches

Weight: 14–18 pounds

Color: silver, apricot, light yellowish brown, black; black mask, dorsal stripe, and black beauty spot on forehead and cheeks

Petit Brabançon (bottom)

Shoulder height: 7–8 inches

Weight: 8–13 pounds

Color: red, black, black and tan, dark mask

The pug is a popular breed. The skin folds on his face have to be cleaned regularly.

Pug

Dutch sailors brought pugs home with them from the Far East. When William and Mary of Orange came to England to be king and queen in 1688, they brought along their pugs and thus introduced them to the English. Until the twentieth century, pugs were kept in royal courts and palaces. As pampered, overweight companions of elderly ladies, they earned a reputation as stupid, lazy dogs. Some defining characteristics are the pug's faithful, bulging eyes; the worry lines on his forehead; and his wheezy pant. He loves treats and can be trained using bribes! Those who can afford to keep him, and give him enough exercise despite his reluctance to run, will get a lot of joy from living with this cheerful, attentive dog. The pug is never aggressive, always in good spirits, relaxed, and never nervous. Unfortunately his extremely short nose does cause him breathing difficulties, especially in warm weather.

Petit Brabançon

Also called the small Brabant griffon, this dog is the descendant of the small Belgian pinscher crossed with a pug. He is a very affectionate little dog that loves to play. As long as he is given plenty of exercise and games, he has a high life expectancy, about twelve to fifteen years. The eye and nose wrinkles must be kept scrupulously clean; he is otherwise an easy dog to care for.

Miniature Bull Terrier

Shoulder height: maximum 14 inches

Weight: 24–33 pounds

Color: all except blue and liver

The miniature bull terrier is a small muscular dog that is easy to care for.

The bull terrier, a former bull baiter and fighting dog, was eventually banned, so the mini bull terrier grew in popularity. His ancestors were the English bulldog and the now extinct white terriers. He was bred to be a show dog from the mid-nineteenth century onward. He is a faithful replica of the bull terrier and has all his good traits. He is friendly, relaxed, and cuddly. He is known for his people-oriented nature. This self-confident, robust, very tough, yet sensitive dog needs consistent training due to his distinctive dominance; even some experienced dog owners will find this a problem, but his miniature size means it is not as serious. He is somewhat docile but barks readily. The naturally fearless dog rarely attacks; however, he will defend anything that has been entrusted to him. He shows a strong

desire to dominate dogs of the same sex. Pure white miniature bull terriers are most likely to be born deaf, and they also tend to have skin problems.

Maltese and Coton de Tulear

Maltese
Shoulder height: 8–10 inches for a male, 8–9 inches for a female
Weight: 6.5–9 pounds
Color: pure white, a pale ivory tinge is permitted

Coton de Tulear
Shoulder height: 10–12 inches for a male, 8.5–10.5 inches for a female
Weight: 9–13 pounds for a male, 8–11 pounds for a female
Color: white; yellow and gray flecks, most often found on the ears, are permitted

These two Bichon breeds require particularly intensive grooming.

Maltese

The most famous Bichon was well on its way to becoming a fashion dog. Fortunately, the grooming proved to be too expensive for most people, so this trend soon fell by the wayside. He was bred on the island of Malta in the Mediterranean, but his true origin is not known for certain. Maltese are lively, docile, intelligent housemates. They love to run around and will happily accompany their human's every step.

The smooth, heavy silk-like, floor-length fur must be combed daily; the eyes cleaned every morning; and the beard cleaned after each meal. The genital area must be kept clean. The fur needs to be washed regularly. This breed is only for those who enjoy grooming and have the time needed to perform grooming rituals religiously. This intensive grooming will ensure his coat is kept in good condition and remains a pure white color. His floor-length fur makes him look like he is floating above the ground when he walks!

Coton de Tulear

Sailors brought his ancestors to the port city of Tulear on the island of Madagascar. His name is derived from *cotton*, because he has cotton-like fur, and his place of origin, Tulear in Madagascar. When groomed, he should resemble a cotton ball, as his name suggests. He is a delightful dog for even the smallest of living spaces. He only has one request—to be with his owner at all times.

Top: two Maltese

Left: a Coton de Tulear

Bichon Frise and Bolognese

Bichon Frise
Shoulder height: maximum 12 inches
Weight: 7–12 pounds
Color: pure white

Bolognese
Shoulder height: 10.5–12 inches for a male, 10–11 inches for a female
Weight: 5.5–9 pounds
Color: pure white

Bichon breeds are very pleasant companions.

Bichon Frise

In ancient Rome, these white dogs were the popular companions of distinguished ladies. The former Tenerife dog, now called the bichon frise, has curly fur, an adorable nature, and is full of charm, wisdom, happiness, and kindness. He is watchful without being noisy and a perfect apartment dog. He loves walks but can sometimes do without. He has the ability to wrap his people around his little paw because it simply is not possible to stay angry with him or resist his affection. The tousled, confident dog must be thoroughly brushed twice a week and bathed once a month. The tips of his corkscrew-like fur, which is similar to that of a Mongolian sheep, need to be cut into shape. The bichon frise is relatively easy to care for, which is reflected by his popularity.

Bolognese

This breed originated from Italy and was the favorite of famous women such as Catherine the Great of Russia and Maria Theresa of Austria. The Bolognese is characterized by his crazy, curly fur. He is a charming apartment dog that loves to stay close to his owner and share his good mood with everyone around him.

Top: a bichon frise

Left: a Bolognese

143

Havanese and Lowchen

Havanese

Shoulder height: 9–10.5 inches

Weight: 7–13 pounds

Color: white, light fawn to brown, black, solid or mottled

Lowchen

Shoulder height: 10–13 inches

Weight: 13 pounds

Color: all, solid or with colored blotches, except brown

The Lowchen was rescued from near extinction in the second half of the twentieth century.

Top: a Havanese

Below: a Lowchen

Havanese

His ancestors came with the Spaniards to Cuba, where they enjoyed a long reign of popularity, but were forgotten during all the political turmoil. Cuban exiles brought them to the United States where they built the breed back up again. The Havanese is intelligent and curious with irresistible charm. Less known is the fact that the breed was once used on the small farms of Cuba as herding dogs. The soft fur needs to be regularly combed and bathed.

Lowchen

The Lowchen, which means "little lion" in German, is traceable to as far back as 1442. They are found in many old paintings, drawings, and literature. His fur is trimmed into the shape of a lion. He is the easiest bichon to care for, even when he is not sheared. He is a lively, cheerful, adaptable dog that likes to exercise and loves his walks. He is alert but not a barker. He is always looking for fun and games and is very affectionate. He loves cuddles and follows his people everywhere. This is not a problem because the "little lion" is open, easy to train, happy, and obedient. He is suitable to keep in both the city and the country and is highly recommended for inexperienced dog owners.

King Charles Spaniels and Kooikerhondje

Cavalier King Charles Spaniel

Shoulder height: 12–13 inches

Weight: 12–17.5 pounds

Color: tricolor, black and tan, white with red plates, chestnut red

King Charles Spaniel

Shoulder height: 10 inches

Weight: 8–14 pounds

Color: same as the Cavalier King Charles spaniel

Kooikerhondje

Shoulder height: 14–16 inches

Weight: 20–40 pounds

Color: white with orange-red patches

These very gentle breeds are suitable for beginners.

Cavalier King Charles and King Charles Spaniels

Their ancestors were Spanish and French flushing dogs, and they were the favorites of English kings, which is where they got their name from. The cavalier almost became extinct because the short-nosed King Charles became the favored breed. But an American saw the cavalier in an old painting and attempted to track down one of these dogs in England. The previously unpopular long-nosed breed now had a market and rapidly grew in popularity, while the King Charles became rare. They are very affectionate, loving, and cheerful dogs that are devoted to their owners. They love walks and enjoy playing in the garden but are not keen on running. They are very sociable and good to keep in a group. The soft fur requires regular grooming.

Kooikerhondje

This dog is a Dutch descendant of ancient flushing breeds that were originally used as working dogs, particularly in duck hunting and tolling (luring ducks close enough to shoot). Today, he is a very pleasant companion dog, whose smooth, long fur is easy to maintain.

Top: Cavalier King Charles spaniels

Below left: a King Charles spaniel

Below right: a Kooikerhondje

Chihuahua and Chinese Crested Dog

Chihuahua

Shoulder height: 6–9 inches

Weight: 1–6.5 pounds

Coat: long and short hair

Color: all

Chinese Crested Dog

Shoulder height: 11–13 inches for a male, 9–12 inches for a female

Weight: 12 pounds

Color: all

Both breeds are ideal companions for elderly and disabled people.

Top: a Chinese crested dog (right), two long-haired Chihuahuas (left and front), and a short-haired Chihuahua

Below left: the "powder puff" variant of the Chinese crested dog

Below right: a short-haired Chihuahua

Chihuahua

There are many myths surrounding the origin of the Chihuahua. They were said to have been around since the time of the Aztecs, time of the Vikings, or are said to be relatives of the small Portuguese Podengos, which were kept on ships as rat catchers during the discovery of the New World. Americans discovered these diminutive dogs in Mexico and bred them to become the smallest dog in the world. Healthy Chihuahuas from good breeding are confident, curious, downright bold, and full of spirit. They should never be nervous or shy. The Chihuahua is intelligent and alert and will assert himself even when in the company of a much larger dog. He is a large personality in a pocket-sized package. His favorite activity is cuddling, and he works very well in a pair. He has a very high life expectancy. The slightly fringed long-haired type is easy to groom.

Chinese Crested Dog

Brought over by sailors from China, these hairless dogs were bred in the United States. There is a pretty variant called the "powder puff." Both types are lively, affectionate, and needy. They are suspicious of strangers and totally devoted to their owners. They are ideal apartment dogs. The hairless type is perfect for dog fans who have allergies to dog fur or who are wheelchair bound.

Continental Toy Spaniel

Shoulder height: about 11 inches

Weight: two categories:
a) up to 5.5 pounds
b) 5.5–10 pounds for a male, 5.5–11 pounds for a female

Color: all colors on a white background permitted

The long fur does not have an undercoat and is easy to groom.

This breed has two different types: the **papillon**, with large, erect, butterfly-shaped ears, and the **Phalène**, with long, floppy ears. In the twelfth century, miniature spaniels were kept by ladies of the Spanish court. In the fourteenth and fifteenth centuries, these dogs were part of everyday life for the majority of European aristocrats.

They were a privilege of the rich and nearly became extinct during the French Revolution. In the nineteenth century, the erect-eared papillons were bred by crossing spitz breeds with the Chihuahua. Today this type is much more common than the Phalène. The papillon is sensitive but should not be a quivering bundle of nerves. He is robust, confident, cheerful, intelligent, and full of character. He is easy to train and is a docile housemate that fits easily into family life, but he should not be considered a toy for a child.

The toy spaniel loves walking. This pleasant apartment dog is just as happy in the city as he is in the country where he loves to chase mice and rabbits. He is suited to miniature agility training. He can be kept as part of a group.

Top: a papillon

Right: a Phalène

147

Pomeranian and Japanese Spitz

Pomeranian

Shoulder height: 7–8.5 inches

Weight: 3–7 pounds

Color: black, white, brown, orange, gray, cream, cream-sable, orange-sable, black and tan, bicolored

Japanese Spitz

Shoulder height: 12–15 inches, females slightly smaller

Weight: 11–20 pounds

Color: white

The huge, fluffy coat requires careful grooming.

Pomeranian

This breed is also known as the dwarf German spitz. At the turn of the twentieth century, this dog found many enthusiastic friends in the United States and England who named him the Pomeranian. This breed is not easy to groom, and the Pomeranians can hardly be called a robust representative of the spitz family. He may be tiny, but he has a large personality and exudes confidence, even when in the company of much larger dogs. He is a popular show dog in Anglo-Saxon countries. The Pomeranian is an adorable, colorful companion for all those who want an intelligent, cheerful tiny dog that is utterly devoted to his owner.

Japanese Spitz

This dog is a friendly housemate, quieter than the German spitz and never aggressive. His face wears the smile of his Asian ancestors. His standard states that he should never be a noisy dog. He is a pleasant companion dog, ideal for beginners.

Top: a Pomeranian

Left: a Japanese spitz

Pekingese and Japanese Chin

Pekingese
Shoulder height: 6–9 inches

Weight: maximum 11 pounds for a male, maximum 12 pounds for a female

Color: all except albino and liver

Japanese Chin
Shoulder height: about 10 inches, the female is slightly smaller

Weight: 4–15 pounds

Color: white with black or red markings with uniform markings on face

Pekingese males should appear tiny; however, they are surprisingly heavy to pick up.

Pekingese

His golden age was during the Manchu dynasty (1644–1912). After the English conquest in Beijing, China, in 1860, only five of them were taken to England. The small dog is very self-confident, daring, headstrong, and never submissive. Gentle, affectionate, and cuddly when he feels like it, he does not give his affection to everyone. He is an ideal apartment dog with little need for running. His fur needs intensive grooming, his large eyes are very sensitive, and his short nose can sometimes cause him breathing difficulties.

Japanese Chin

Korean rulers gave these palace pooches to Japanese emperors as gifts. They were only kept by the highest nobility, lived in bamboo cages, and were carried around in large kimono sleeves. They arrived in England in 1853 as gifts. Chins are lively, cheerful, and playful well into old age. They love long walks, are easy to train, and are tenderly devoted to their owners. The long coat is not difficult to groom, but the eyelids need to be cleaned regularly.

Top: a Pekingese

Left: a Japanese chin

Shih Tzu

Shoulder height: maximum 10.5 inches

Weight: ideal 10–16 pounds

Color: all

With proper care and maintenance, the Shih Tzu has a high life expectancy.

The Chinese called him *Shi-tze-kou*, which means the "Tibetan lion dog." He belongs to the lion dog breeds of the Far East, which is closely associated with the teachings of the Buddha, and his appearance is supposed to represent the lion. The precious temple pooches arrived at the Chinese court as gifts, where they were bred with a lot of love and care, and presumably this is where they developed their short noses. The first ones arrived in England in 1930 and were initially named Chinese apsos. He is suspected to be a relative of the Peking Palace dog due to their physical similarities. He was eventually recognized as a separate breed. He is a robust small dog with an exuberant temperament and friendly character. His distinctively charming personality has been preserved over the centuries. He is a very good apartment dog that loves walks but is just as happy to play in the garden. The cheerful Shih Tzu is playful well into old age. The long, lush fur needs intensive grooming but his fur can be trimmed if he is not a show dog.

Lhasa Apso and Tibetan Spaniel

Lhasa Apso
Shoulder height: ideal 10 inches, the female is slightly smaller

Weight: 13–15 pounds for a male, the female slightly less

Color: gold, fawn, honey, dark grizzle, slate, smoke, two-tone, black, white, or brown

Tibetan Spaniel
Shoulder height: about 10 inches

Weight: ideal 9–15 pounds

Color: all

Tibet, located in the Himalayas, is called the "roof of the world."

Lhasa Apso

This breed was the favorite dog of the aristocracy in ancient Tibet and is still a treasured and respected member of the family. The Tibetan apsos are seen as "little people." Nuns and monks who misbehaved were said to be reincarnated as Lhasa apsos. The Lhasa is rather suspicious of strangers but affectionate and tender toward his family, while still retaining his proud personality. He is a cheerful housemate who loves long walks. He is very robust and has a high life expectancy. The lush, long fur, which was once protection against the extreme climate of his homeland, is floor length and very maintenance intensive. Those who do not wish to exhibit their dogs can keep the fur short.

Tibetan Spaniel

The lion pup lived in monasteries for the edification of the monks and was trained to turn the prayer wheels. According to legend, the dog was able to transform himself into a lion when the Buddha was in danger. He was therefore held in high esteem. The Tibetan spaniel is a tough, adaptable, cheerful, lively, and intelligent member of the household that does not like strangers but is utterly devoted to his family. However, this self-confident dog needs to be trained with plenty of love from an early age. He has a high life expectancy.

Top: a Lhaso apso

Below: a Tibetan spaniel

Miniature Schnauzer and Affenpinscher

Miniature Schnauzer

Shoulder height: 12–14 inches

Weight: about 9–17.5 pounds

Color: black, white, salt and pepper, black and silver

Affenpinscher

Shoulder height: 10–12 inches

Weight: 9–13 pounds

Color: pure black with black undercoat

The robust personality makes this dog fun for beginners.

Miniature Schnauzer

Miniature schnauzers and affenpinschers are breeds that are often associated with each other. They were the companions of fine ladies as well as coach and stable dogs that caught rats and mice. In 1899, these dogs were separated into two breeds. Instead of the round-headed, short-nosed dwarf form, breeders aimed for a smaller version of the schnauzer. The fearless daredevil knows how to bluff larger dogs by using his self-confidence. His lively temperament and loud, joyful barking is not for those of a nervous disposition. He needs consistent training so he does not wind his family around his little paw. He is mistrustful of strangers, sometimes even unfriendly, but he is loyal to his family. He is a good companion for elderly or single people. His mustache needs to be trimmed regularly, but he does not shed very much. He is a cheerful, jolly dog who loves to explore.

Affenpinscher

This breed has a dislike of strangers and can sometimes be quick tempered. He is loving toward his people but can be rather grumpy and has a strong personality. This small dog is easy to care for and makes an ideal apartment dog. He is just as happy in the city as he is in the country. He loves long walks and has a high life expectancy.

Top: a black and silver miniature schnauzer

Left: an affenpinscher

Miniature Pinscher

Shoulder height: 10–12 inches

Weight: 9–13 pounds

Color: solid deer red, reddish brown, black and red

The reddish brown miniature pinscher is also known as the Rehpinscher.

The miniature pinscher and miniature schnauzer were around even before pure breeding of schnauzer and pinscher breeds began. The miniatures were popular parlor dogs. They were the companions of aristocratic ladies at the turn of the century and could never be small and delicate enough. Happily, the breeding ideal did not aim for a small, delicate, trembling lapdog, but one which looked exactly like a pocket-sized pinscher. The features of the typical toy dog—a round head, small pointed muzzle, large, protruding eyes—are just as unwanted as an anxious character. He is adaptable and follows his family everywhere. He is an ideal companion for an elderly person and loves company and affection. He is playful, funny, tender, and confident. This docile little dog is easy to train and loves to be cuddled. He is an incorruptible guard dog and is naturally suspicious of strangers. The miniature pinscher's coat is smooth and easy to care for. He is an ideal apartment dog and for people who want to take their dogs everywhere with them. However, he should not live in extreme climates. This tiny, robust dog has a long life expectancy of about fifteen years or more.

Portuguese Water Dog
and Labradoodle

Portuguese Water Dog (right)

Shoulder height: 19.5–27.5 inches for a male, 17–20.5 inches for a female

Weight: 42–55 pounds for a male, 35–48.5 pounds for a female

Coat: curly or wavy

Color: black, white, or brown, with or without white

Labradoodle (bottom)
*Not recognized by FCI

Shoulder height: 21–25 inches

Weight: 51–66 pounds

Color: yellow, brown, black, spotted

Labradoodles are often called "designer dogs."

Portuguese Water Dog

The wise, strong, robust Portuguese water dog is an excellent swimmer. He helped to drag in nets and boats and other equipment from the water. On the high seas, he sent messages between boats and was an indispensable aid of the seafaring Portuguese. Thanks to his high intelligence and affable nature, he is now a popular family dog that can be easily trained and is cheerful and alert without being aggressive. He is sheared according to his traditional shape. He needs plenty of exercise and meaningful tasks.

Labradoodle

Originally a cross between a poodle and a Labrador retriever, he was intended as a guide dog for blind people with dog allergies. The open-minded, friendly, intelligent breed is a pleasant family dog. Anyone who has a dog allergy yet wishes to own a dog would do well to acquire one of these because he does not shed and aggravate allergies. He is an active dog who needs plenty of exercise and meaningful tasks. Labradoodle fur is very maintenance intensive.

Elo® and Wäller

Elo
*Not recognized by FCI

Shoulder height: 18–23.5 inches, *small Elo:* 14–18 inches

Weight: 48.5–77 pounds, *small Elo:* 22–33 pounds

Coat: smooth and wirehaired

Color: all colors, white spotted preferred

Wäller
*Not recognized by FCI

Shoulder height: 21.5–25.5 inches for a male, 19.5–23.5 inches for a female

Weight: about 66 pounds for a male, about 57 pounds for a female

Color: all

The small Elo is a result of crossing smaller Elos with miniature spitz and Pekingese.

Elo

He has been known as the "practical family dog" in Germany since 1987 due to his calm, moderate temperament; he rarely barks and rarely exhibits hunting behavior. He is playful, alert but not aggressive, friendly with children and other dogs as well as other animals. He is a result of a crossing between the Old English sheepdog, the chow chow, and the Eurasier. This family dog needs consistent training because he knows his own mind. His smooth coat is easy to care for; the wire-haired type needs intensive grooming.

Wäller

This newly created German breed has existed since 1994, and his breeding goal was a sporty, straightforward dog that is easy for beginners to look after. He is a family dog with long fur that is easy to care for and was a result of a crossing between the Briard and Australian shepherd. He is friendly toward other dogs, pets, and especially loves children.

Both breeds are bred carefully by their own breeding clubs in order to produce dogs with the desired characteristics.

Top: an Elo

Left: a Wäller

Kromfohrländer

Shoulder height: 15–18 inches

Weight: 24–35 pounds for a male, 20–31 pounds for a female

Coat: smooth and rough

Color: white with brown patches

The two different types should not be bred with one another.

Top: a rough-coated Kromfohrländer

The Kromfohrländer, or Krom dog, came about as a happy accident: a female fox terrier took a liking to a dog called Tin Tin belonging to a soldier in 1945. Tin Tin was allegedly a Breton griffon. The result was a litter of delightful crossbreeds that were taken on by Ilse Schleifenbaum. Their pretty appearance, cheerful nature, and robust health delighted her so much, she decided to breed them. She asked for the assistance of an experienced dog expert, and the Kromfohrländer became a recognized breed in 1955. *Krom fohr* means "crooked furrow," an area in their homeland near Siegen, Germany. Krom dogs only have a small group of devoted fans, and the puppies are brought up in a close community with humans. They are open minded, love people, and are affectionate family dogs. They tend not to stray or hunt and love long walks. They remain playful well into old age and are easy to train and keep busy. Krom dogs are sociable and can be kept in a group. These alert dogs are not aggressive but tend to flash their teeth when threatened. The grooming is straightforward for both types.

Further Reading

Books

American Kennel Club. *The American Kennel Club's Meet the Breeds.* Irvine, Calif.: BowTie Press, 2012.

Hall, Derek. *Ultimate Guide to Dog Breeds.* Wigston Leicester, England: Lorenz Books, 2010.

Morgan, Diane. *Complete Guide to Dog Breeds: Everything You Need to Know to Choose the Right Dog for You.* Neptune, N.J.: TFH Publications, 2013.

Internet Addresses

American Kennel Club
http://www.akc.org

Animal Planet: Dog Breed Selector
http://animal.discovery.com/breed-selector/dog-breeds.html

Fédération Cynologique Internationale (World Canine Organization)
http://www.fci.be/

A–Z List of Dog Breeds

Translated from the German edition by Claire Mullen.

Edited and produced by Enslow Publishers, Inc.

Originally published in German.

© 2006 Franckh-Kosmos Verlags-GmbH & Co. KG, Stuttgart, Germany

Eva-Maria Krämer, *Hunderassen: Die 200 beliebtesten Rassen*

Library of Congress Cataloging-in-Publication Data

Krämer, Eva-Maria.
  [Hunderassen. English]
  Get to know dog breeds : the 200 most popular breeds /
  Eva-Maria Krämer.
    p. cm. — (Get to know cat, dog, and horse breeds)
    Summary: "Discusses the appearance, origin, and
    temperament of more than two hundred dog breeds
    categorized into groups according to the tasks they were
    originally bred for, including herding dogs, hunting dogs,
    sled dogs, lap dogs, and more"— Provided by publisher.
  Audience: 011-
  Audience: Grades 7 to 8.
  Includes bibliographical references and index.
  ISBN 978-0-7660-4258-2
  1. Dogs—Juvenile literature. 2. Dog breeds—Juvenile
    literature. I. Title.
  SF426.5.K7313 2014
  636.7'1—dc23
                    2013007011

Paperback ISBN 978-1-4644-0459-7

Printed in the United States of America

112013 Lake Book Manufacturing, Inc., Melrose Park, IL

10 9 8 7 6 5 4 3 2 1

To Our Readers: We have done our best to make sure all Internet addresses in this book were active and appropriate when we went to press. However, the author and publisher have no control over and assume no liability for the material available on those Internet sites or on other Web sites they may link to. Any comments or suggestions can be sent by e-mail to comments@enslow.com or to the address on the back cover.

Every effort has been made to locate all copyright holders of material used in this book. If any errors or omissions have occurred, corrections will be made in future editions of this book.

All information in this book is given to the best of the author's knowledge. However, care during implementation is still required. The publishers, authors, and translators assume no liability for personal injury, property damage, or financial loss as a result of the application of the methods and ideas presented in this book.

♻ Enslow Publishers, Inc., is committed to printing our books on recycled paper. The paper in every book contains 10% to 30% post-consumer waste (PCW). The cover board on the outside of each book contains 100% PCW. Our goal is to do our part to help young people and the environment too!

Photo Credits: Photographs by Eva-Maria Krämer except Heike Erdmann/Kosmos, p. 5 (top); Magdalene Grenz, p. 4; Thomas Höller/Kosmos, pp. 7, 8 (top), 93 (left); Christof Salata/Kosmos, pp. 6, 8 (bottom), 9; Wolfgang Siegel, p. 45 (top right); Karl-Heinz Widmann/Kosmos, p. 5 (bottom).

Cover Photo: Shutterstock.com (*main photo:* Labrador retriever; *from top to bottom:* German shepherd, beagle, Pomeranian, Chihuahua).